THE PACIFIC NORTHWEST SEAFOOD COOKBOOK

SALMON, CRAB, OYSTERS, AND MORE

THE COUNTRYMAN PRESS
A division of W. W. Norton & Company
Independent Publishers Since 1923

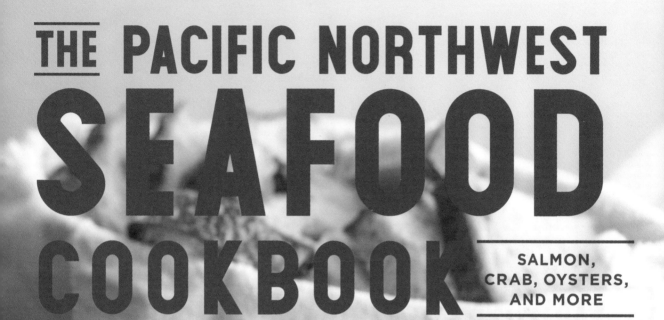

THE PACIFIC NORTHWEST SEAFOOD COOKBOOK

SALMON, CRAB, OYSTERS, AND MORE

NAOMI TOMKY

PHOTOGRAPHY BY CELESTE NOCHE

For information about permission to reproduce selections from this book, write to
Permissions, The Countryman Press, 500 Fifth Avenue, New York, NY 10110

For information about special discounts for bulk purchases, please contact
W. W. Norton Special Sales at specialsales@wwnorton.com or 800-233-4830

Manufacturing through Imago
Book design by Anna Reich
Production manager: Devon Zahn

The Countryman Press
www.countrymanpress.com

Library of Congress Cataloging-in-Publication Data

Names: Tomky, Naomi, author. | Noche, Celeste, photographer.
Title: The Pacific Northwest seafood cookbook : salmon, crab, oysters, and more /
    Naomi Tomky ; photographs by Celeste Noche.
Description: First edition. | New York, NY : The Countryman Press, a division of
    W. W. Norton & Company Independent Publishing since 1923, [2020] |
    Includes index.
Identifiers: LCCN 2019020283 | ISBN 9781682683668 (hardcover)
Subjects: LCSH: Cooking (Seafood)—Northwest, Pacific. | LCGFT: Cookbooks.
Classification: LCC TX747 .T617 2020 | DDC 641.6/92—dc23
LC record available at https://lccn.loc.gov/2019020283

A division of W. W. Norton & Company, Inc.
500 Fifth Avenue, New York, NY 10110
www.wwnorton.com

10 9 8 7 6 5 4 3 2 1

FOR BRETT, MY FAVORITE DISHWASHER,
SEAFOOD-EATER, AND PERSON

CONTENTS

SHELLFISH

128

Growing up in Seattle, walking around Pike Place Market by age eight as if I owned it, and eventually becoming a food writer—none of this translates directly to understanding or loving seafood. Though it seems that perfectly cooked salmon should be my birthright and I ought to have stirred chowder with my teething toys, the reality is that Seattle's pristine seafood remains something of a mystery to many lifelong residents, as well as to newcomers and visitors.

In the '80s, salmon was often "that stinky fish a friend's uncle caught." Tossed on the grill until dry and stuck on like glue, it hardly inspired anyone to go out and pay good money for it. Still today, for many home cooks, that memory lingers: of mishandled or overcooked fish, improperly prepared oysters, or the unsolved mystery of how to cook a crab.

An overhead look at oysters growing at Chelsea Farms in Olympia, Washington

All of this adds up to an intimidating proposition: seafood, especially the high-quality goods of the Pacific Northwest, leans pricey. The fragile fish need to be cared for and cooked quickly after purchase. The margin of error is thinner for seafood than for a thick, resilient cut of meat, but the reward is also better. Perfectly cooked fish is sublime: bursting with clear saltwater flavor, tender, and rich with buttery fat.

Consider this book your roadmap to achieving that result: starting from that first panicked moment in the store, wondering if a piece of fish is even good. Does it deserve that price? How do you know it's not past its prime? This book will hold your hand while you purchase the fish, help you keep it fresh at home, and then walk you through cooking it, from the first foolproof recipes—like the Slow-Roasted Salmon on page 49—to stunning dinner party centerpieces, like the Pacific Northwest version of Moqueca, the Brazilian seafood stew, on page 224.

It's a path that I traveled myself in the not-too-distant past. Despite growing up in the Pacific Northwest, aside from the occasional clam feast (as I mention in the Steamed Clams recipe on page 174), seafood wasn't an everyday part of my life. When I moved back to my beloved hometown of Seattle after college, though, I saw seafood through new eyes.

While making little money but many friends in the advertising department of a local newspaper, I started with a deep dive into happy hours—especially the Seattle tradition of oyster happy hours. For as little as 25 cents apiece, we could slurp oysters as quickly as we could order them, wandering out into the night hours later, sated with the dozens downed.

Soon after this, I began working for a group of restaurants. My office sat above the kitchen of a seafood restaurant, where the smell of crab cakes frying often influenced my lunch decisions. There I met the late, great Jon Rowley, the city's guiding seafood spirit, as he brought the first Yukon River keta salmon to market—not knowing I'd later follow him through mushroom fields and across oyster flats to witness just a glimpse of his culinary expertise.

During a later job at a catering company, I stepped into the kitchen when staff was shorthanded, happily shucking, grilling, or frying oysters as needed, until I could do it quickly, expertly, and without gouging my hand with the oyster knife. I worked for a frozen seafood company, learning the mass-market side of the business: taste-testing year-old fish sticks to see how far into the future we could realistically claim they were "best by," and then taking home mountains of deeply discounted product. Laying out a tablecloth of newspapers, I'd text friends to come over with bread and wine and we'd crack crab long into the evening, until our hands were slippery with butter, clumsily trying to pick the shell shards from the carpet.

By the time I became a full-time food writer, telling the stories of Seattle's notable foods, best chefs, and most intriguing culinary stories, seafood had won my heart. I championed the city's shellfish in national magazines, flaunted the region's impeccable fish in guidebooks, and shared the stories of the people who catch and cook it wherever I could.

Because what I learned, through all the years of wide-eyed, open-mouthed observation, was that while we have access to an impressively grand spread of sustainable wild and farmed seafood here in the Pacific Northwest, we don't have widespread knowledge of how to cook it.

We go out to eat salmon and halibut, we regularly sidle up to oyster bars and slurp up mussels, but cooking seafood at home is a relatively rare event. This book tries to change that. It aims to bring the bounty of the Pacific Northwest not only into local home kitchens, but also into the kitchens of visitors who have tasted the local bounty and want to re-create those flavors at home. Which brings me to my final question in shaping the direction of this book and the types of recipes I wanted to include. Beyond the creatures from our local waters: what is Pacific Northwest seafood as a cuisine?

The Pacific Northwest I grew up in—the one where I still live—

thrives because of its people, which is exactly what I aim to capture in this cookbook. You will find a variety of recipes, from the historic and groundbreaking—like Shiro Kashiba's black cod (page 108) and Tom Douglas's insight on wild salmon (page 54)—to the lesser-known but no less important takes on local seafood—a recipe from an Iraqi refugee, converted to local lingcod from the river fish she knew growing up (page 112), and Native American chef Hillel Echo-Hawk's squid recipe using pre-colonial ingredients (page 236). This book incorporates the flavors of Seattle that I grew up with—including Filipino food I ate at friends' parties and Thai curries from my favorite restaurants—and the flavors I discovered on my travels, but have brought back and adapted to the Pacific Northwest, like the Albacore Tacos (page 93).

What I learned during this process is that living in the Pacific Northwest makes you think about your food. From our forests to our coastlines and oceans, we are surrounded by lush abundance. From British Columbia down to Oregon, the combination of saltwater coastline, islands, rivers, and freshwater lakes, as well as mountains and old-growth forests, not only produces amazing seafood, but also calls on us to think a little bit harder about why and how we eat it.

The region's seafood, fish, and shellfish long sustained Indigenous peoples hunting and gathering along the coasts and inlets. Over decades of immigration, diverse cultures have come together to create a cuisine that is as varied as its inhabitants, yet still specific to this particular place.

Pacific Northwest cuisine means exceptional quality and thoughtful preparation. And, to be honest, a fair amount of fennel. It means inclusivity—of ingredients, techniques, and traditions. Even if—no, especially if—that means you don't have any experience with the food at all, we want you to join us at our table. This book is written to share the Pacific Northwest with everyone; to bring the PNW flavor home. To celebrate both the bounty of fresh seafood and the blending of culture and cuisine, through recipes ranging from traditional favorites to the interesting, unexpected, or international twists found in the region today.

Welcome. Take a deep breath, and let's dive into cooking seafood. As I mentioned in the Introduction, cooking seafood can be intimidating because the product is often expensive, buying decisions can be fraught (Which fish? How much? How long will it last?), and many of the simpler ways to cook meat or vegetables are trickier with fish. The idea behind this book is to walk you through each step: to help you buy the right fish, store it properly, and then cook it in a way that matches your skill level.

Each chapter begins with the easiest recipe—what I like to call my "foolproof" recipe. It has plenty of margin for error if you get distracted or aren't sure if you took it out of the oven or off the heat in time. You *probably* could mess this recipe up, but you'd have to be actively trying (please don't try). If you're anxious about cooking with seafood, you might want to start with this recipe before moving on to later recipes, which might be more challenging for new seafood cooks.

But before you get started, I offer a few suggestions, recommendations, and clarifications.

CHEF RECIPES

About a third of the recipes in this book aren't mine: they were generously entrusted to me by professional chefs, restaurateurs, local cookbook authors, and amateur cooks in the region. Everyone who cooks with seafood in the Pacific Northwest has a slightly different culinary outlook, and bringing in their recipes helps to capture that diversity. Whenever you see a name under the recipe title, that's the cook who created it—and who has carved out their own worthwhile niche of Pacific Northwest seafood. For those with a restaurant (or more than one) as of the writing of this book, I've provided the name so that you can taste the chef's dishes at the source.

PORTION SIZES

The portion sizes in the book are small—very few of the dishes here will be a full meal. They are meant to be a main dish, a side, or an appetizer, accompanied by rice, noodles, vegetables, or whatever else you like to eat. Most of the main dishes here use 1 pound of fish for four people (or an equivalent amount of shellfish)—smaller than the 6- to 8-ounce portions you might be used to seeing in other books or at restaurants, but also cheaper (and, should you be buying pre-cut fillets, an easy weight to find). If you're feeling flush and hungry, you can always double the recipe. And, as with meat, more and more people treat fish as one component of a meal, rather than as an enormous entrée—a move that is good for pocketbooks and fish stocks alike.

SPECIAL EQUIPMENT

The single item I mention in this book more than anything else is a thermometer. An **instant-read thermometer** that can check the internal temperature of your fish, as well as the temperature of your oil for any frying, will do more to prevent you from over- or under-cooking your fish than any time guideline or visual cues I can offer in each recipe. They cost as little as $10 for a basic digital one, and you'll use it all the time—for this book and other cooking projects.

In terms of pots and pans, you'll mostly want to avoid non-stick for ideal fish cookery, and often you will want heavy-bottomed pots. I use my **cast-iron pan** and **enameled cast-iron Dutch oven** for most of the fish cooking I do.

People like **fish spatulas**—and they will make your life somewhat easier, especially for the crispy skin that everyone loves and for whole fish, like the Trout with Spring Pea Salsa Verde (page 125). But if you don't have one, it's not the end of the world.

It will be the end of the world—or, at least, it'll make your life much more difficult—if you don't have a set of **tweezers** handy. They don't need to be anything special, though a set that is big enough to use your whole hand (as opposed to the little ones from a Swiss Army knife) is helpful. They make removing pin bones and debearding mussels infinitely easier.

If you're planning to shuck your own oysters, you *will* need an **oyster shucker**. My first time bringing home oysters, I used a screwdriver, and while I managed to survive without impaling myself, you might not be so lucky. Most fish stores sell these; you can grab one as you pick up your oysters.

A few other things you'll find useful to have around as you cook your way through: a **spice grinder** (I use an old coffee grinder, highly recommended) or mortar and pestle, and a **microplane** or similar tool for zesting citrus.

INGREDIENTS AND INSTRUCTIONS

I've tried to keep the ingredients lists limited to products you'll find in your standard grocery store, since you may already be going to a second location for the fish. Nearly everything that doesn't fit that category is cheaply and easily available online, though you may need to plan ahead a bit.

Anytime I mention an herb, it's assumed to be fresh rather than dried, unless specified.

Finally, I use the phrase "as needed" often, mostly with salt, pepper, and occasionally oil. I prefer this to the traditional "to taste" as some of the time you won't be tasting. I encourage you not to worry about this—I use it in places where you will not ruin a dish if you over- or under-salt. Generally, I use it when asking you to salt or pepper a fillet. Because a fillet of the same weight may be a different shape or size, there's no exact amount of salt and pepper needed and my estimate is unlikely to be any more accurate than yours. For a standard pinch amount, grab salt between your thumb and forefinger, hold your hand over the fish and rub them together, letting it rain down on the fillet. Yes, that's the right amount, you did perfectly. Now please don't stress about it.

Finally, there is one thing that goes incredibly well with fish, is used a number of times throughout this book, and is not readily for sale: pickled shallots. They are, however, extremely easy to make. Make them, keep them in your refrigerator, and use them often.

QUICK PICKLED SHALLOTS

1 cup white wine vinegar

2 tablespoons sugar

2 tablespoons kosher salt

1 tablespoon black peppercorns

3 to 4 shallots sliced thin (ideally with a mandoline)

Bring the vinegar and ½ cup of water to a boil in a small pot. Stir in the sugar and salt until they're dissolved, then add the peppercorns. Pack the shallots loosely in a 16-ounce jar (or two smaller ones) and pour the liquid over them. Cover and store in the refrigerator for at least 5 hours and up to 2 weeks.

Okay, you've decided to cook fish. Now what? How do you know what to buy? Where to buy it? If it's fresh enough or worth the price tag? Is it okay to buy frozen fish? In this section, you'll learn where to buy your fish and what you should ask to make sure you're getting a good product.

WHERE TO BUY SEAFOOD

The first step to cooking seafood with confidence is to buy the right product from the right place. Remember: It's in the fishmongers' best interest for you to successfully purchase, cook, and eat their product—that's the only way they get a repeat customer—so they generally will be a good source for information.

The next thing to know is that it's okay to ask questions. Most fishmongers are excited to help you get interested in fish—they know the ins and outs of not only the product, but also how to cook it. My local shop, Wild Salmon Seafood Market in Seattle, has info sheets with recipes and instructions behind the counter, but there's even deeper knowledge to be found any time you ask someone a question.

In buying the fish you need for the recipes in this book or any other, you should know your priorities. For me, the top priority is sustainability: if I eat this fish now, can I eat it again, and can my children and grandchildren enjoy it as well, all without destroying the environment? Then, I want to make sure that the fish or shellfish was raised or caught in a humane and careful way, before finally figuring out if it's the right fish for the recipe or a usable substitute.

Asking these questions is easiest to do in a seafood market or fish shop—in Seattle, we're lucky to have quite a few good ones, including Wild Salmon Seafood Market, Mutual Fish Company, and Kuzma's Fish Market, along with the ones in Pike Place Market, such as Pure Fish Market—but the seafood counter at any grocery store should be staffed with folks who know their stuff. If they don't, consider going elsewhere.

Many farmers' markets have seafood vendors, too. Much like buying the freshest vegetables direct from the people who grow them, buying fish at a farmers' market sometimes means you can meet the person who caught your fish or dug for your clams. They will know even more than the fish shop about its sustainability and the methods used to catch it, plus you know that you are supporting local fishing economies.

Another option is purchasing direct online—this is a particularly good option if you visited the Northwest and have now returned home but miss the flavors of the region. With high-quality freezing methods (more on that in a moment) and overnight shipping, everything from live oysters to stunning salmon can land on your doorstep in the same condition that we buy it in Seattle. Look for the same keywords and information on the website that you'd ask for in a shop—you can check out companies like Sena Sea Wild Alaskan Fish, Taylor Shellfish Farms, and Lummi Island Wild to see how it's done. Many Seattle shops (including Wild Salmon Seafood Market and Mutual Fish Company) offer overnight shipping to customers around the country.

SUSTAINABILITY

The United States has strict fishery regulations for commercial fisheries. In the most basic of terms, if a wild fish is caught in the United States, it can be considered sustainable. That wasn't always the case, but consumer demand for sustainable seafood, coupled with a new generation of fishermen who are aware of the need to be responsible in their work, has turned the tide (pun intended) for most seafood that originates from the United States. According to the National Ocean and Atmospheric Administration and as of the writing of this cookbook, 91 percent of the seafood caught in the United States is fished at sustainable levels. That said, it's important to be up to date on what you should or shouldn't be eating. The Monterey Bay Aquarium's Seafood Watch program (seafoodwatch.org) is the easiest and most comprehensive source for quick checks on what is or is not sustainable: the app, pocket guides, and website include nearly every fish you will find and list them as "Best Choice," "Good Alternative," or "Avoid."

Even with all the research that goes into the Monterey Bay Aquarium's seafood cards—they produce different cards for different regions of the country—they are not the be-all-and-end-all source on sustainability. There are exceptions to the rules, especially when considering sustainable seafood. You can always ask your fisherman at the farmers' market or fishmonger about specific fish if you are unsure—often if it seems that a high-quality shop is selling something that isn't widely considered sustainable, it's because they have a niche provider doing something exceptional, or the information has changed since Seafood Watch put out that guideline. At a shop that doesn't specialize in seafood, it's best to use more caution and stick to the published information—but if you're buying wild-caught American seafood, you're usually going to be fine.

FARMED VS. WILD

If you read the sustainability section above, you might notice my careful use of "wild" to describe American seafood that you can count on to be sustainable. Farmed versus wild fish can be a bit confusing: farmed salmon is bad, but farmed trout is good. And farmed shellfish is great! What's the difference?

Basically, it comes down to where they grow and where they go. Shellfish farms grow their product in the exact same place the oysters, clams, or mussels would grow in nature (the filter feeders even help clean up their environment). But while wild salmon are on the move—from their natal stream down to the ocean and back—farmed salmon stay in one place. That means waste, uneaten feed, and uneaten medication pile up in one place. Meanwhile, if the farmed salmon get an infection or parasite, it's treated by the farmer—but the nets don't pen in the diseases, and it can spread to the wild salmon nearby that don't get treated.

The reason that farmed trout don't run into these issues is because they are farmed via low-risk closed containment systems, meaning that there is a barrier between the fish farm and the natural environment—either on land or using raceways, which divert water from natural streams, and water can be monitored and filtered to keep it clean.

So it's not that all farmed seafood is bad; it's just that nobody has successfully made a safe, sustainable system for farming salmon yet. Until they do, avoid farmed salmon.

QUALITY

When it comes to seafood, freshness is often equated with quality, but it's important to talk about what that means for live shellfish, fresh seafood, and frozen fish—and what else contributes to the quality of your seafood. And beyond that, how can you judge the quality of the fish you see for sale?

For each type of live shellfish, freshness has a different measure. I provide recommendations in the individual chapters, but here are a few general guidelines.

It may come as a shock, but flash- or deep-frozen fish will almost always be the best form to purchase to ensure high-quality seafood. If you're able to head down to the albacore docks in Oregon or buy a salmon straight off the boat in Seattle, you might match or beat the quality of frozen fish, but for the most part, the best fish is treated the best—and that means it's carefully handled, bled, and frozen on the boats when caught (known as frozen-at-sea, or FAS), kept frozen throughout its journey to the shop, and sold to you either still frozen or carefully thawed.

Sena Wheeler, whose Sena Sea Wild Alaskan Fish sells salmon, black cod, and halibut online (senasea.com) and at Seattle farmers' markets, explains that deterioration starts as soon as a fish has landed on board the boat, so that every minute before it's chilled counts against the quality of the fish.

"As a kid, I didn't even know what 'fishy smelling' meant," she says, because properly cared-for fish or shellfish—frozen or fresh—should smell only of the sea. But how do you check for that? At some fish shops, they might be able to hold up the product for you to smell and/or feel. There should not be a scent beyond saltwater, and a gentle poke on the skin side should result in the skin bouncing back.

If you can get only a visual on the fish, here are a few things you can look for: the meat side should be smooth and flush—no dents or discolorations, which indicate mishandling. The meat should be tight to the skin and the bones, without gaping or holes at the pin bones. Fish vary in color, but look for the desired color—it's okay for lingcod to have a blue-green tinge, but beware of any yellowing in halibut. As a general rule, though, color should be even throughout—no bruises or blood spots. But again, there is the exception to the rule! In the Pacific Northwest you may run across a marbled Chinook salmon, meaning it has a blend of pink and white flesh. If you see this fish, scoop it up as it is hard to find and a local favorite. Marbled Chinook will cook to an even color and taste just like its red schoolmates.

If you're buying a whole fish, the eyes are—as they say—a window to the soul: make sure they are prominent and not receding into the fish (a sign that the flesh is deteriorating, no longer fresh and taut).

For live shellfish, the tests tend to be a bit easier: is it alive and properly cared for? If so, then your main mission is to purchase it as close to harvest date as possible. All shellfish is sold with a harvest tag, which has the exact location and date it was harvested—be very suspicious if a shop refuses to show you that tag. For mussels, you'll want to buy them within two or three days of harvesting and eat them within a day, but clams and oysters are a bit hardier and can last up to two weeks from harvest if properly cared for—though you'll still want to eat them within a few days of purchase. Crabs and spot prawns kept in live tanks are best purchased quickly after they're brought in (two or three days, maximum), as they lose fat (and thus quality) once out of the wild.

Check your live shellfish for signs of life: they should be intact (make sure your crab has all ten of its legs) and their shells should not be cracked or broken. For mussels and clams, if they are open and you tap them or squeeze them, they should clamp shut. Oysters, on the other hand, should be tightly closed: if they are open, they are dead and not edible.

For oysters on the half-shell, you'll always want to use live oysters that you shuck as you need them. But for cooked preparations, like the Oyster Stew on page 202, you can use jarred, shucked oysters that can be found in the refrigerated section or packed in ice at the seafood counter—just check the date they are packed, make sure they smell sweet and briny once opened, and try to eat them within 10 days of the "packed on" or "shucked on" date.

Purchase clams, mussels, and pink scallops only if they are alive (unless you're buying a processed version: tinned, smoked, or canned in a sauce). For spot prawns, you'll see them live (head-on), and fresh or frozen (usually head-off, except in rare cases). When buying non-live spot prawns—fresh or previously frozen—make sure that they feel firm, are free of black spots, and smell of the sea with no hint of ammonia. Buy live and you will have the freshest prawns. Should one or two die before you cook them, check to see if they pass the sight and smell test described above.

Oregon pink shrimp (sometimes sold as bay shrimp) are sold cooked and can often be found in the freezer section. Dungeness crab is either live or cooked. In the case of both cooked shrimp and crab, they should be treated like fish: the quickness of the freezing is most important for the quality of the product.

HOW TO STORE SEAFOOD

Now that you've bought your fish and shellfish, you want to take good care of it. If you've purchased frozen fish or shrimp, the storing is easy: keep it in your freezer. To defrost your frozen seafood, unwrap it and place it in on a rack in a pan deep enough to catch any liquid that may come off as it defrosts. You never want your fish (frozen or fresh) to sit in its own liquid. Marinades: good; fish drippings: bad. Place the pan with the fish on the lowest shelf of your refrigerator—overnight should be plenty of time for it to defrost. When it's defrosted and you're ready to cook, pat it dry and proceed with your prep work. If you really want to use your fish that night, seal it in a zip-top plastic bag with all the air pushed out of it and set it under cool running water until it's defrosted.

For fresh fish or fish that was previously frozen but that you purchased already thawed, simply remove the fish from the packaging, pat it dry, and re-wrap it tightly in plastic. Keep it in the coldest part of your refrigerator.

For live bivalves (your oysters, clams, scallops, and mussels), spread them in a single layer on a baking sheet or similar, and then cover them with a damp towel—like a kitchen rag that you've wet and wrung out—and store in the refrigerator. If you won't be eating them within a day or so, make sure to rewet the towel so it stays damp.

For live spot prawns or crabs, hopefully you'll be cooking them soon so there isn't much storing, but keep them in the coldest part of your refrigerator until you're ready to cook or kill them.

Throughout the world, nearly every hunter-gatherer society roamed their home region, moving with the animals and the harvest. The Indigenous people of the Pacific Northwest serve as the exception to the rule: with the plentiful salmon runs, bountiful berries, and myriad other resources, the Coast Salish and their brethren had no reason to move about. The food came to them.

The Pacific Northwest, pre-contact (before the arrival of European or other non-Indigenous settlers), was the largest, most densely populated non-agricultural land in the world. Locals ate dozens of different plants, from the huckleberry to the wild carrot, hunted birds and mammals, and, of course, caught more than 30 kinds of fish and harvested nearly as many shellfish—including all the kinds in this book. Mainly, though, the Coast Salish and other Northwest Coast Indians lived on fish.

Since its beginnings 10,000 years ago, the Native diet of the Northwest has changed. But their food remains the original cuisine of the Pacific Northwest, and when we, as guests on the land and sea, learn to cook using the same resources they've long treasured, we follow in their footsteps.

Sadly, we can't always follow a direct path: many of those traditions have been quelled by the exploitative history of exploration and settlement in the region. The identity of the first non-Native to sail onto local shores is up for debate. Some say it was a Chinese adventurer named Hwui Shan, who crossed the Pacific in 458 CE; others say the first non-Native to arrive didn't show up until the parade of Europeans a millennium-plus later, which included, possibly, a Greek named Apostolos Valerianos—better known by his Spanish name, Juan de Fuca—who gave descriptions of foreigners rolling up what may have been the strait now named for him, and the British pirate Francis Drake, who made it to Oregon in 1579. But it is a known fact that British captains James Cook and George Vancouver were the first Europeans to chart Puget Sound, in the late 18th century.

By the time Meriwether Lewis and William Clark reached the mouth of the Columbia River in 1805, they were hardly the first explorers to trample the Native lands. Smallpox and other diseases introduced by Europeans had already begun to destroy the Native populations and traditions. But the journals of Lewis and Clark offer some of the first descriptions of rolling up the Columbia River and encountering Native people and their foods: "Large scaffolds of fish drying at every lodge," wrote Clark. "Piles of salmon." He described the river as "remarkably clear and crowded with salmon in many places." They describe, extensively, how much dried and pounded fish they found.

As America turned westward, following Manifest Destiny—the belief that the United States should stretch from coast to coast—the Pacific Northwest began to gain population, eventually declaring a provisional government in 1843. But it wasn't until after 1850—when about 1,000 settlers lived there—that the non-Native population really began to explode.

Not long after President Millard Fillmore established the Washington Territory in 1853, the Indigenous tribes were conned and sometimes forced to trade their land for fishing treaties. The agreements promised the tribes full fishing rights in exchange for their land. But as the population skyrocketed, those rights became useless. By 1860, the Washington Territory had almost 12,000 inhabitants. Commercial fishing fleets grew in huge numbers, thanks to advances in canning processes, and they chased the salmon farther and farther out to sea, preventing the fish from returning to their spawning sites—and the Native fishing areas.

Meanwhile, the Pacific Northwest began to grow up. The city of Seattle was formed in 1865 and incorporated in 1869; by the following year, the territory had more than 20,000 people. The new salmon canning industry depended heavily on Chinese immigrants. The Chinese workers, first arriving in the 1870s, soon established their own neighborhood—what is still today known as Seattle's Chinatown/International District. The Japanese workers who followed often came with families, which led to the adjacent Japantown—where Maneki, a Japanese restaurant founded in 1904, still stands. The first Filipino workers arrived as early as 1911, with larger numbers coming in the 1920s, with the goal of education, though they often ended up working in the canneries as well. All three groups brought with them knowledge of the seafood of their own home countries and wove it together with the fish and shellfish found in the Pacific Northwest—influences that are still on the table today.

In 1909, Seattle hosted its first world's fair, the Alaska-Yukon-Pacific Exposition, attracting 4 million people and establishing Seattle as a major regional player. The region's seafood was already widely served in restaurants—the menu of Drake's Restaurant from 1911 offers salmon bellies served to order, clam chowder, fried halibut, fried or boiled salmon, and fried smelt (maybe similar to the ones on page 242). The wide availability of stewed calves' brains and raisin pie may have changed, but the clam chowder remains. The Maison Blanc in 1920 offered a menu of the region's seafood not unlike the chapters of this book: halibut, black cod, salmon, trout, smelt, crab, oysters, and shrimp—plus a few left out of this book for sustainability reasons, such as abalone.

Seattle's iconic, historic market opened on Pike Place in 1907, making it now the oldest operating farmers' market in the country. While it started out selling produce, by 1917 the city of Seattle had a fish problem: prices were skyrocketing and supply was low. The governor stepped in and a municipal fish market opened, selling fish and oysters at a third the previous cost. Even with sales limited to 3.5 pounds per person, it sold almost 1,400 pounds of salmon alone on its first day. Soon after, the municipal market converted to a privately owned business, a fish stall that still stands in Pike Place Market (now called City Fish), along with a few other fish shops—including, yes, the place that throws the fish (Pike Place Fish Market).

The Pike Place Market has been a haven for immigrant entrepreneurs—first Japanese and Italians, later Sephardic Jews. Wholesale change swept through the market during World War II, as America interned entire local Japanese communities in camps. Few of the many Japanese-owned businesses survived the horrific policy.

Scandinavians—who brought with them yet another fish-focused cuisine—manned the fishing fleets out of Ballard, and in 1938, Ivar Haglund opened the first Ivar's Seafood Restaurant, selling clam chowder and fish and chips on his way to becoming a local icon. In 1950, Peter Canlis opened his namesake restaurant perched over Lake Union and began serving the Canlis prawns still on the menu today.

In 1962, Seattle again hosted a world's fair, with the towering Space Needle as its centerpiece. Dinner at the top of the Needle featured shrimp cocktail, Olympia oysters, and Dungeness crab legs as appetizers, while mains included fillet of Puget Sound salmon with lemon butter, or, on Fridays, "Rainbow trout from the surrounding streams and rivers." The event also created Tillicum Village on Blake Island, aiming to educate visitors about Native culture—with a salmon barbecue. A bit hokey, but a big step. The fair featured a "Food Circus"—which in retrospect isn't an appropriate name for an old armory building that showed off cuisines of the world—Thai, Japanese, Mexican, Chinese, German, and more. It expanded the culinary world for locals and gave a boost to already estab-

lished shops like Uwajimaya, the Japanese grocery chain that still runs some of the best fish counters in the region. Another Japanese influence arrived shortly thereafter: Shiro Kashiba, whose signature recipe for black cod appears on page 108, brought Edo-style sushi to town—at one point going to work at Maneki, that longtime staple of Japantown.

As the region grew, however, a problem brewed: Native American fishing, a right signed into the treaties of the 1850s, was becoming criminalized. A century after the agreements, Native fishermen were still being denied their rights to fish here, and as the Civil Rights movement swelled around the country in the mid-1960s, in Washington State it took the form of the Fish Wars, during which Native fishermen demonstrated and protested against the denial of their treaty rights. The 1974 Boldt Decision in the US District Court was eventually affirmed by the Supreme Court and allowed treaty fishermen not only half of potential harvests, but also equal voice in fishery management.

The region's boom-bust economy kept moving forward, welcoming immigrants who knew as well as locals what to do with the seafood found here. In the '70s and '80s, Vietnamese immigrants started arriving. Hmong flower farmers added color to the flower stands of Pike Place Market and restaurateurs introduced the city to phở and myriad other flavors of their homeland, an influence that pervades seafood restaurants around the city: a shrimp bánh mì here, lemongrass steamed clams there, and local versions of chả cá Lã Vọng with black cod or rockfish all over the place.

In 1989, Tom Douglas opened Dahlia Lounge and started a new era of Northwest cooking, gaining national fame for showcasing local seafood in a diverse array of flavors and techniques—including grilled salmon, like the recipe he provided for this book on page 54. He trained his chefs impeccably in the art of salmon and local specialties, and many of them went on to find their own fame—like John Sundstrom, whose mussel recipe is on page 216. Douglas led the Seattle culinary world onto the national stage, and did so with an eye toward advocacy including fair treatment of his employees and the sustainability of the seafood he used and still uses at his now 16 restaurants.

Today, it seems hard to imagine the Pacific Northwest's food scene not being tightly tied to the seafood caught and harvested nearby, but even Seattle's urban partner in the region, Portland, Oregon, hasn't quite caught up in the breadth of restaurants and availability of product.

Where do we go from here? The best way to keep improving the seafood scene—in Seattle, in Portland, and wherever you might be reading this—is to seek out the best, most sustainable products, cook them in delightful, stress-free ways, and serve them to friends and family. To enjoy a good meal of fish and shellfish in a local restaurant or in your own home is to spread the word of great seafood and of Pacific Northwest cuisine.

FISH

SALMON:
ICON OF
THE REGION

Shining, silvery salmon have long been the symbol of the Pacific Northwest. It's the first thing people think of when the region's cuisine comes up in conversation and the longest-lasting memory of what they ate when they visited. And for good reason: it's ubiquitous, cherished, and adored here.

Fresh-caught and flash-frozen salmon is sold at every grocery store's seafood counter, from stalls at every farmers' market, and even from the side of boats at Fishermen's Terminal. It is not hard to locate Seattle's stunning fish for your own use, and it's even easier to turn it into your next meal.

On the scale of intimidation, salmon score high—the same things that make it taste so good when done right make it easy to overcook: high fat and delicate texture. Often newbies looking to cook salmon think that the easiest way to do it is to just toss it in a pan—but this isn't a steak, and cooking it like one is tricky. Instead, start with the slow-roasted version on page 49, and let yourself fall in love with the silky orange layers, and big, rich flakes. Use the leftovers for Salmon Chowder (page 56) or Salmon Salad (page 51), and never again be the person who microwaves fish at the office.

Salmon is high maintenance only if you let it be—buy a few affordable fillets at the farmers' market, keep them in the freezer until an hour before dinner, then quick-defrost and slow-roast, setting a spectacular table with a dinner party–worthy dish, and you'll have a very different outlook.

CULTURE AND CUISINE OF THE SALMON PEOPLE

For the Coast Salish tribes, whose native land includes most of the Pacific Northwest, salmon are the center of the universe. Their creation stories, their legends, and their folklore speak to the importance of salmon to their existence.

"The new generation is coming now and you shall be food for the people, O Dog Salmon," Moon said, as he began changing the earth in the legend of Moon the Transformer. Snoqualmie Charlie (sia'txted) told this story to an anthropologist in 1916, when he was around 65 years old. "The first thing he transforms, to prepare the world, is salmon," explains Roger Fernandes, an artist, storyteller, educator, and member of the Native American tribe of the Lower Elwha Band of the S'Klallam. "Salmon is the center of the world."

As buffalo are to the Plains tribes, salmon are to the Pacific Northwest tribes: the center of their diet, religion, lore, and natural world. Like food in general in the region, the fish were abundant. For generations, the people here made dugout canoes and hunted for salmon and the other fish described in this book, as well as whales and seals. They wove fishing nets from plants and carved fish hooks from tree bark. They smoked and dried fish in ways still used today—both by Native peoples and adapted to non-Native restaurants, as in the Cedar Plank–Grilled Salmon on page 52. In great wooden longhouses—like the Duwamish one in West Seattle today—they sang and danced and gave each other food, sharing the wealth of the salmon people among the village.

Today, Northwest Native peoples continue to share the wealth of salmon: local tribes are among the biggest contributors (both in money and effort) to the restoration of salmon habitat in the region. But the cuisine of the Pacific Northwest has changed in the years between when Dog Salmon was put in the river to be food for the human world and today.

Salmon runs considered "pre-contact" (before 1850) were likely 10 to 20 times what we see today in the Pacific Northwest. Canneries opened immediately after non-Native settlers arrived, with 272,000 pounds shipping out annually from the Columbia River by 1866. From 1900 to 1919, more than 1 million cases of canned salmon left Washington each year. Soon after that, efforts to prevent salmon population reduction began—even as large-scale dams like the Bonneville and Coulee were built, drastically impeding the ability of fish to return to their natal streams and destroying the elements of the habitat salmon require to spawn the next generation.

Planting hatchery fish, requiring fish ladders on dams, limiting fishing, and other efforts have fought the man-made destruction of salmon habitat (due to huge population growth and climate change). The results of these efforts have allowed the continuation of sustainable Tribal, sport, and commercial fishing of salmon in much of the Pacific Northwest, even as concerns about other runs, such as the Chinook returning to Puget Sound, continue.

Lore has it that when European settlers first arrived in the Northwest, the Native people refused to sell them salmon for fear it would not be treated with respect—and they were likely correct. But today, Washingtonians vote and rally for the removal of dams like the Lower Elwha (built in 1911 and removed between 2011 and 2014) and the Glines Canyon (built in 1927 and removed the same time as the Lower Elwha). There are many more dams around the Pacific Northwest slated for the same, which will hopefully move salmon populations back in the direction of the teeming pre-contact population numbers.

SALMON TYPES

Salmon is a many-splendored thing. It's also a many-species thing, with a proliferation of names that could mean nothing to you or could get your taste buds dancing as they dream of the fatty fish. The recipes here don't specify which type of salmon you need because, really, they will all work for any of them. However, it's good to understand why you might choose one salmon over another so that you can be prepared to buy whatever is in season and will work for you.

As I discuss in the trout section, steelhead is somewhere between a salmon and a trout, and will work for many of these recipes as well (for steelhead, check current sustainability information before purchasing), as will Arctic char. Do not purchase Atlantic salmon: it is farmed, unsustainable, and frankly flavorless. Stick to wild salmon. It's available fro-

zen year-round, and while the bulk of it comes in fresh from late spring through early fall, there are runs that keep going nearly all year.

While the names below are the types of salmon, you may also run into a few specialties like Copper or Yukon River, Neah Bay, or Fraser: these are named for where they were caught. Some—like the Copper River Salmon—are trademarked and have stringent standards for the people catching and processing them, while others are just the name of the location. Within each of these places, you'll find a few or all of the five types of salmon.

Pink: Sometimes called "humpy" for the humpback that the males get on their back, they are the region's most abundant salmon—though you're least likely to find them in stores. The small size and mild flavor of pinks mostly pave a path straight to the salmon canneries. When you can find a fillet of this salmon available, cook it gently to appreciate its delicate flavor.

Keta: Often called chum or dog salmon, this was long considered subprime eating—rumor spread that it was called "dog" because that was who should eat it. In fact, the name comes from the large "teeth" that the males grow during spawning, and this fish can be quite good, especially when pulled from longer and colder rivers. This is a great affordable option for dishes where the flavor might come from a sauce rather than from the fish itself, or for people who are hesitant to dive into the big flavors of a king or sockeye. Not as high in fat as other salmon, this fish should be cooked for slightly less time than other species.

Coho: Getting into the more commonly seen types, this one, also known as silver, is considered one of the best for smoking. It's still a little milder flavored than king or sockeye, but it has a longer, later season, often stretching into fall, and a firm, orange-red flesh, great for dishes that will benefit from a meatier texture—like grilling or smoking.

Sockeye: Named for its red flesh—sockeye is a poor transliteration of "suk-kegh," the Coast Salish word for red—it is valued for its brightly hued meat and rich, oily flesh. Sockeye are often considered the best salmon for eating, the Goldilocks of big flavor and firm texture. Like the coho, it works well on the grill, but also is perfect for the slow-roasted recipe on page 49.

Chinook: King salmon, the largest and most distinguished species, gets big flavor from the fattiness, something that fish-lovers appreciate, but which can be a bit overwhelming for newbies. That said, it makes for a great pan-searing or baking option, as the abundant oils keep it from drying out, which gives the cook a slightly larger margin of error.

HOW TO FILLET SALMON

The best answer to "how to fillet a salmon" is to ask your fishmonger to do it. You can skip straight down to the next section to learn how to remove pin bones. But, should you have somehow come into the salmon through an alternate fashion—you caught it yourself (nice job!),

 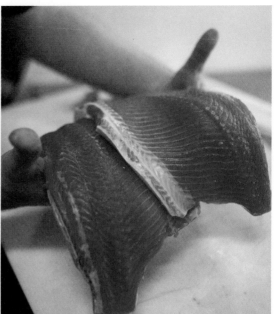

purchased it from a back alley (not recommended), or were given it—you can pretty quickly and easily fillet it yourself. It probably won't look as nice as when the pros do it—it's definitely a learned skill—but just save your scrap meat for a Salmon Chowder (like the one on page 56) or Pot Pie (page 53), and you'll still make the most of the whole fish.

Place your fish on a plastic cutting board with a non-stick mat or wrung-out wet towel underneath to stabilize it. Use scissors to clip off the fins. Slice the fish down the belly (underside) from the vent (er, anus) forward and remove all the innards, including (in a female) the roe sac. (You can cure the roe by removing the eggs from the membrane and soaking them in a mixture of soy sauce, sugar, and salt for about 24 hours.)

Then pick up the fillet knife. If the head is still on, you'll want to remove that. Because it tends to degrade quickly, that's often already done, even if you're buying whole fish. Slip your knife just behind the neck and cut through on one side. Flip to the other side and repeat, then push the knife hard through the bone to take the head all the way off.

Cut the fillet from the fish, slicing from the head to the back, starting each long stroke just above the spine and cutting toward the belly, keeping the knife angled inward. Use long, smooth movements to cut the fillet off, keeping as close to the spine as possible. When you get to the tail, cut perpendicular to the fish, so you can remove the fillet. Pull the fillet away from the spine and use your knife, blade toward the fish, to pull the rest of the meat away from the ribs. Flip the fish and repeat on the other fillet. Trim the fillet—you can use the little pieces and edges in the pot pie and chowder as well. You can also use a spoon to scrape the meat off the backbone and do the same with that meat—or grill the skeleton whole and flake off remaining meat for a pre-dinner snack.

HOW TO REMOVE PIN BONES AND SKIN

Now you're ready to remove the pin bones. If you run your hand over the flesh of the fillet or lightly scrape with the back of your knife, you'll feel the pin bones. They run in a straight line down the salmon, so if you pull them while the fillet is whole, it's a bit easier than after you've portioned it out. Use a pair of tweezers and, like plucking an eyebrow hair, pull gently in the direction it's pointing.

If you want to remove the skin, start at the tail end and slip the knife between the skin and the flesh. Then angle the knife just about 30 degrees up from the cutting board and press down gently, holding the skin down with your other hand, as you move the knife horizontally. Keep the skin to make a salmon version of the Halibut Chicharrones on page 87.

SLOW-ROASTED SALMON

SERVES 4

The word "foolproof" gets tossed around a lot when it comes to recipes, but rarely when it comes to temperamental proteins like tender salmon. When shelling out money for a good side of wild Pacific Northwest salmon, nobody wants to take chances, though, and this *truly* foolproof method of cooking leaves it beautifully bright, intact, and never dried out.

This recipe works well for any size portion: simply adjust the oil, salt, and lemon amounts to the size of the salmon. The timing stays the same and you should have plenty of chimichurri.

1 pound skin-on salmon, pin
    bones removed
1 tablespoon olive oil
¼ teaspoon kosher salt
¼ lemon
Chimichurri Sauce, to serve
    (recipe follows)

Preheat the oven to 225°F. Rub both sides of the salmon lightly with the olive oil, then sprinkle the salt on top. Place the salmon skin side down on a baking sheet and bake for 20 minutes. Don't worry too much about exact timing, as the recipe is very forgiving. When the salmon is done, it may still look uncooked, as the color doesn't change much, but don't worry: it's cooked. Small dots of white fat may bubble up, but they are nothing to be concerned about (fat is flavor!). Remove the salmon from the oven and squeeze lemon lightly over the top. Serve as is or with a sauce of your choice—like the chimichurri that follows.

recipe continues

CHIMICHURRI SAUCE

In Argentina, this parsley-based sauce comes out at every *parillada*, or grill feast. But the sharp vinegar, piquant pepper flakes, and fresh herbs also work well with fish dishes like this one. Because you can make it ahead of time, it turns the salmon into a low-stress dinner party stunner. For any portion of salmon less than a pound, you'll have enough left over for a second meal—simply store it in the refrigerator and use it over pasta, eggs, or shrimp.

3 garlic cloves

2 tablespoons white wine
    vinegar

½ cup olive oil

½ teaspoon kosher salt

½ teaspoon red pepper flakes

½ cup flat-leaf parsley leaves

1 tablespoon oregano leaves

Mash the garlic (use a garlic press, if you have one; otherwise crush it with the broad side of a knife or mince it fine) and stir it together with the vinegar in a small bowl. Slowly whisk in the olive oil, then add the salt and pepper flakes. Chop the parsley and oregano fine, then put them into a mixing bowl and pour in the oil mixture, stirring well. You can save on chopping time and make this in the food processor, with but a small loss of texture.

SALMON SALAD

SERVES 2 FOR LUNCH OR 12 AS AN APPETIZER

Leftover salmon has the reputation of, well . . . old fish. Nobody wants to be the person who microwaved the stink into the office all day and there are few ways to warm it up while preserving the gentle texture of most fish. But dishes like this salmon salad show that leftover seafood is more about rethinking than reheating. It makes a good work lunch eaten on saltines or similar crackers, but also works well as an hors d'oeuvre on crostini or in a butter lettuce cup.

1 medium cucumber, diced

Kosher salt

1 cup cooked and flaked skinless, boneless salmon (see note)

¼ cup dill, chopped

½ cup crème fraîche

Freshly ground pepper

Sprinkle the cucumber with salt and let it drain on paper towels or in a colander for 10 minutes. Gently stir together the cucumber, salmon, dill, and crème fraîche. Season with pepper and salt, to taste.

If starting from scratch, cook a hefty ½-pound salmon using the slow-roasted method on page 49, then flake it. Either way, don't stress too much on the amount of salmon—this is meant to use up the leftovers, not be a precise measurement!

CEDAR PLANK–GRILLED SALMON

SERVES 4

Sitting on our back deck one summer, we suddenly saw a flaming slat of wood sail off our neighbor's patio, landing in the grass, where it was quickly pursued by our neighbor—with a gushing hose. That's not an altogether uncommon sight in Seattle, where cedar plank grilling is a tradition, adapted from the smoking methods of the Native people in the Pacific Northwest. Using cedar or alder sticks, the traditional method kept the fillets vertical, a few feet above the fire, leaving the meat juicy and full of flavor. The method changed a bit as it was brought inside by restaurant chefs, then back out by home cooks giving it a shot.

The key to this recipe, though, as my neighbors learned, is to soak your wood plank before putting it on the grill—I recommend two hours, minimum.

1 tablespoon brown sugar

2 tablespoons unsalted butter, melted

½ tablespoon white wine vinegar

1 pound skin-on salmon, pin bones removed, cut widthwise into 4 long, thin fillets

Kosher salt, as needed

Soak the cedar plank for 2 hours.

Heat the grill to medium-low (about 350°F) with indirect heat—that means pushing all the coals to one side so you can place the fish on the other side. For gas, turn on half the grill and you'll put the plank on the other half.

Stir the brown sugar into the butter until it's incorporated, then add the vinegar and mix well.

Salt the salmon fillets and place them skin side down on the cedar plank, making sure that there is a little room between each fillet and that each is entirely on the board.

Brush all showing sides of the salmon with the butter glaze.

Place the plank over indirect heat on the grill. Let the fillets cook for about 10 to 12 minutes, until just done—you can check with a thermometer, the internal temperature should be 120°F.

SALMON POT PIE

SERVES 4 TO 6

So often fish is treated delicately, but it doesn't have to be: the big flavor of salmon stands up well to the comfort food stylings of a pot pie. By adding the salmon after simmering but before baking, it cooks lightly and gives its essence to the rest of the dish.

3 tablespoons unsalted butter

1 large carrot, halved lengthwise and sliced

1 leek, white part only, halved lengthwise and sliced

1 celery rib, sliced

3 garlic cloves, chopped

1 teaspoon kosher salt, plus more as needed

1 head broccoli florets (about 4 cups if buying pre-cut)

2½ cups chicken stock

3 sprigs thyme leaves

¼ cup all-purpose flour

½ pound salmon, skin and bones removed, cut into bite-sized pieces

1 sheet puff pastry (see note)

1 egg, beaten

Freshly ground black pepper, as needed

Preheat the oven to 400°F.

Heat the butter in a large pot over medium heat. Add the carrot, leek, celery, garlic, and 1 teaspoon of salt and cook, stirring, until the vegetables start to soften, about 5 minutes. Add the broccoli florets and keep cooking until they're bright green and beginning to soften, about 3 minutes.

Add the chicken stock and the thyme leaves, bring to a boil, and then turn it down to a low heat to simmer for about 10 minutes.

Use a slotted spoon to remove the bulk of the vegetables from the soup (you can put them in your baking pan for holding so you don't dirty an additional dish). It doesn't need to be perfect; you just need them out of the way for a minute. Slowly whisk the flour into the remaining stock, trying to stir out any lumps.

Remove the pot from the heat and stir the vegetables back in, also adding the salmon, then pour into an 8-inch square baking dish. Cover the dish with the puff pastry (you can really just sort of set the pastry on top of the dish). Brush the pastry with the egg, then sprinkle generously with salt and pepper.

Bake the pie for 20 to 25 minutes, or until the puff pastry is a golden brown and just starting to darken in spots.

I use a store-bought puff pastry to make this pie because it's easy and works well, but if you're ambitious and comfortable with pastry, feel free to make your own.

GRILLED SALMON WITH FENNEL AND CHARRED TOMATO RELISH

SERVES 4

TOM DOUGLAS | TOM DOUGLAS RESTAURANTS | SEATTLE

Tom Douglas didn't invent cooking with wild salmon, but he has been one of its most prominent advocates. Douglas, Seattle's original celebrity chef, opened the Dahlia Lounge in 1989 and has been charming the scales off local seafood ever since. And he hasn't served a lick of farmed salmon in any of his restaurants since about 2001. "Here's the thing," he says. "In order to save the remaining salmon supply, we must eat wild to save wild." His recipe here shows how to do it with simple, fabulous flavor—and will help you grill fish without letting any of it stick to the grate.

½ pound medium tomatoes, ripe but firm, cored and cut in half

1 yellow onion, thickly sliced

1 poblano or Anaheim chile, split in half horizontally, stemmed and seeded

Juice of ½ lemon

½ teaspoon minced garlic

Pinch of ground cayenne pepper

1½ tablespoons olive oil, plus more as needed

2 tablespoons chopped fresh herbs (such as chives, tarragon, fennel fronds, or a mixture)

Kosher salt, as needed

Freshly ground black pepper, as needed

1½ tablespoons fennel seeds

1½ tablespoons flaky sea salt (such as Maldon)

1 pound skin-on salmon, pin bones removed, in 4 fillets

4 lemon wedges

Heat the grill to medium (about 400°F), then put on the tomatoes, onion, and pepper halves. Let them blacken, turning them carefully as needed, until charred. Transfer them to a cutting board and chop coarsely. Scrape them into a bowl, then add the lemon juice, garlic, cayenne, and 1 tablespoon of olive oil.

When the vegetables have cooled to room temperature, add the herbs and season with kosher salt and pepper to taste.

Crush the fennel seeds using a mortar and pestle or by moving the bottom of a small heavy pot, rolling the edge back and forth over the seeds. Mix the fennel with the sea salt.

Brush the remaining ½ tablespoon of olive oil onto both sides of each salmon fillet and then season both sides with the fennel and salt mix.

Using tongs, oil your grate well by swabbing it with a paper towel drenched in oil.

Grill the salmon skin side down near the edge of your heat, not directly over the coals. When the salmon is marked by the grill on the first side, use a spatula to flip it to the other side and cook until it's done to your liking. Keep an eye on the salmon to make sure it doesn't burn, moving it to a cooler part of the grill if necessary. Aim for an internal temperature of about 125°F if you have a thermometer, about 5 to 8 minutes total grilling time, depending on the thickness of the fillets.

When the salmon is cooked, remove it from the grill and place it on plates. Garnish each piece of salmon with some of the charred tomato relish and a lemon wedge.

A MESSAGE FROM TOM DOUGLAS

Eating wild supports the wild salmon industry and creates an economy around managed fishery environments. If we don't create the economy, we're not going to save the fish.

There's really no reason to use farmed salmon as far as I'm concerned: farmed salmon undermines a healthy habitat and hurts the wild stock, and undercuts the price of fish, which makes wild salmon seem so expensive. This is why I only eat wild salmon and choose to serve wild salmon at all of my restaurants.

SALMON CHOWDER

SERVES 4 TO 6

Clam chowder may get all the press, but this one-pot salmon version embodies the ethos behind Pacific Northwest seafood: a stunning, soul-warming dish with the fish as the star of the show. It's dead simple to make, but the flavors are exciting and lively. There are no tricks or trickiness to the recipe, and it works equally well with the fresh salmon called for here, canned salmon, or leftover cooked salmon. Either way, the result is a comforting, delightful soup that emphasizes the flavor of the fish.

4 ounces bacon, chopped

2 celery ribs, chopped

1 leek, white parts only, chopped

½ teaspoon kosher salt, plus more as needed

1 tablespoon all-purpose flour

2 large Yukon Gold (or similar) potatoes, diced

2 cups chicken stock

2 bay leaves

1 sprig thyme

½ pound salmon, skin and bones removed, cut into bite-sized pieces

1 teaspoon Dijon mustard

½ cup heavy cream

Zest of 1 lemon

¼ cup chopped parsley

In a heavy pot or Dutch oven over medium heat, cook the bacon until most of the fat is rendered and the pieces begin to crisp, about 8 minutes. Add the celery, leek, and ½ teaspoon of salt, and cook, stirring occasionally, until the vegetables are soft, about 5 minutes.

Dust in the flour, stirring to make sure there are no clumps, then add the potatoes, stock, bay leaves, and thyme. Lower the heat and let simmer for 10 minutes. The potatoes should be starting to soften—you should be able to stab them easily with a fork. If not, keep simmering for a few more minutes.

Add the salmon and mustard, and let cook for 3 to 5 minutes, until the salmon is fully opaque. Turn off the heat, stir in the cream and the lemon zest, then salt to taste.

Garnish with parsley.

PAN-SEARED SALMON WITH BASIL AND MINT

SERVES 4

Crispy skin and tender flesh sometimes act like magnetic opposites—if the skin shatters, the fish is over-cooked, and if the fish is perfect, the skin is limp. To find the space in the middle is the ultimate balancing act, but with a little prep and plenty of careful attention, you can get there. Start when you're shopping: this recipe will work better with the thicker parts of the fillet, closer to the head.

1 pound skin-on salmon, pin bones removed

Kosher salt, as needed

Freshly ground black pepper, as needed

2 tablespoons vegetable oil

3 tablespoons olive oil

¼ cup mint leaves

¼ cup basil leaves

Pat the salmon skin dry with a paper towel, then drag the back of a knife across it to dry the skin completely. Refrigerate the salmon, skin side up, for 1 hour.

Remove the fish from the refrigerator, slice into four fillets, and sprinkle generously with salt and pepper. In a stainless steel or well-seasoned cast-iron pan (or anything that is not non-stick), heat 1 tablespoon of vegetable oil over high heat until smoking.

Pour that oil off and heat the second tablespoon of vegetable oil until very hot, then place the fish in, with the skin side down. Gently push down with a fish spatula, as the salmon will try to curl up, resulting in the skin losing contact with the hot pan. This will get splattery—be prepared, and use a splatter screen if you have one. Again, practice patience, staying the course until most of the fish is opaque and the fish lifts easily from the pan, likely about 3 to 4 minutes. If you encounter any resistance, leave it a little longer.

Flip the fish and let it cook on the non-skin side for barely a minute. If your skin slides off as you do this, just set it on top of the fish (like a garnish): it's still crispy! Again, the fish should lift easily. Transfer the fish to a plate, skin side up, to rest for 1 more minute.

While the fish rests, heat up the olive oil in a medium pan over medium heat, add the herbs and stir until they relax, about 1 minute. Drizzle the herbs and oil over the fish and serve.

WHY NOT NON-STICK?
Non-stick pans can be great for keeping things like eggs from cementing onto the pan, but when it comes to cooking crispy-skin fish, you'll want to avoid them. Not only is the kind of super-high heat needed to cook the fish skin not very good for the pan (it will deteriorate much faster), the fish will never get as crisp as it will using a cast-iron or stainless steel pan.

SALMON SINIGANG

SERVES 4

ERLINDA BELTRAN AND CELESTE NOCHE

As we were wandering through Pike Place Market, admiring fish and shooting photos for this very cookbook, Celeste (the photographer) and I got into a conversation with one of the fishmongers. While sinigang—sour soup—is a classic Filipino comfort food dish, the fishmonger argued that salmon sinigang was specifically a West Coast Filipino-American dish. Celeste had some doubts about that, but she also had the confidence that wherever its roots, her mom had a killer recipe for it—so obviously I had to ask to include it in the book.

The dish is also an excellent way to use up the head and tail of a whole salmon—the bones in the soup give it extra flavor. Ask your fishmonger: they likely have some heads and tails sitting around, even if you're not up for buying a whole salmon. If you are, see the instructions on page 45 for how to break it down into fillets, and use the body for this.

2 tablespoons vegetable oil

1 medium yellow onion, sliced
thin

3 garlic cloves, chopped

2 to 3 medium tomatoes, diced

1 inch ginger, julienned

2 tablespoons miso paste

Kosher salt, as needed

Head and tail of 1 salmon (or
1 pound salmon fillet, skin
removed, cut into 2-inch cubes)

2 tablespoons tamarind
concentrate

1 bunch Chinese mustard greens,
chopped across the stem in
1-inch chunks (about 2 cups;
see note)

1 bunch radishes, halved or
quartered (about 1½ cups)

1 jalapeño, stem removed, but
otherwise whole

Cooked rice, to serve

This version of sinigang uses
radishes and mustard greens, but
it can be made with all kinds of
vegetables—Filipinos often use
eggplant, okra, daikon, kangkong,
and string beans.

In a pot large enough to hold the salmon, heat the oil over medium-high heat. Sauté the onion and garlic until the onion starts becoming translucent, about 6 to 8 minutes, then add the tomatoes, smashing them a little, until they break down a bit. Add the ginger and miso and lower the heat to medium.

Lightly salt the fish.

Add 3 cups of water to the pot and bring it up to a boil, then reduce to a simmer before adding the fish. Once it begins to boil again, add the tamarind and stir, then throw in the mustard greens and radishes. Let it come to a boil once more, add the jalapeño, and then turn off the heat. Season with salt to taste.

MISO-CURED SALMON

SERVES 8 AS AN APPETIZER OR BAGEL TOPPING

ROBIN LEVENTHAL

Before moving to Walla Walla, Washington, to teach at the Wine Country Culinary Institute, Robin Leventhal owned Seattle's brunch scene with Crave, located on Capitol Hill. Later, she showed off her skills on Bravo's cooking competition show, *Top Chef*. Her simple salmon cure makes for a smokeless stand-in for lox that requires no special equipment. She suggests serving it on a bagel with goat cheese and pickled red onion, adding it to omelets or scrambled eggs, or presenting it as an appetizer with pickled cucumber on rice crackers.

This needs to be made 24 to 48 hours before serving.

¼ cup white miso paste

2 tablespoons honey

1 tablespoon sesame oil

1 tablespoon soy sauce

2 inches ginger, grated (about
    1 tablespoon)

2 large garlic cloves, minced

Zest of 2 lemons

½ cup kosher salt

½ cup sugar

1 pound skin-on salmon fillet,
    pin bones removed

In a blender or small food processor, add the miso, honey, sesame oil, soy sauce, ginger, garlic, and lemon zest. Puree until it's smooth, then add the salt and sugar and blend just enough to incorporate.

Use two rectangular pans that are large enough to hold your fillet and nest together; the bottom one will need at least a ½-inch-deep rim to catch juices. Coat the first pan with an even layer of the miso cure as a base. Place the salmon fillet skin side down, on top of that layer of cure, then smear more cure over the top of the fillet so both sides are completely covered in it.

Cover the fish with plastic wrap and then place the other dish on top of the salmon. Weigh it down with heavy objects, like canned goods. Aim for even distribution.

For a 1-inch thick salmon fillet, it will take about 24 hours; for a 2-inch fillet, it will be more like 48 hours. Flip and redistribute the cure about halfway through. Check for doneness: fish should be slightly translucent, but not hard. Slice off a piece and taste—it should have the texture of lox.

When your fish is done curing, rinse it well under cold water and pat dry.

To serve, slice with a very sharp, thin blade almost horizontal to the cutting board, aiming for a paper-thin cross-section of the grain, instead of slicing straight down to the board. Freezing the fillet for a few minutes before cutting can help with getting thin slices.

Store the salmon in the refrigerator and use within five days or freeze it, sliced or whole, for later use.

THREE PEPPERCORN POTTED SALMON

SERVES 10 TO 12 AS A SNACK

In discussing Pacific Northwest seafood, it's easy to focus on the most beautiful, fresh, and fattiest of fish. But reality sometimes brings us subpar fish—whether because of affordability or accident. This dish uses ample clarified butter to cover imperfections of taste, and three colors of peppercorn to gloss over any unsightliness. Because the dish comes from a preservation tradition, this also works well to keep fish that might be on the verge of going bad for an extra week or two.

This recipe adds color and flavor through three peppercorns—the traditional black, the unripe green, which add a slightly fresh flavor, and the stunning pink, which aren't actually peppercorns at all, but add a hint of spice. If you can't find green or pink peppercorns, it works fine with just the black pepper (increase the quantity accordingly), but it's more visually interesting and complexly flavored with all three.

I prefer to let the salmon (and, more importantly, the butter) come back to room temperature before serving. Spread it on warm toast points and garnish with cornichons to make this into a fancy appetizer. For a less fancy one, simply spread it on saltines. This is a great make-ahead dish for parties: it will last at least 10 days in the refrigerator, or a few months in the freezer—just let it come back up to room temperature before serving.

recipe continues

1 teaspoon each of green, pink, and black peppercorns

Kosher salt, as needed

1 pound salmon, any type, any condition (bones and skin can remain on, and scraps work for this, which can often be found cheap at your local fish market)

2 cups dry white wine

Juice of ½ lemon

2 tablespoons chopped dill, plus 2 sprigs

1 cup clarified butter (see note)

2 tablespoons capers

Clarified butter or ghee is often available on store shelves, but can also be easily made from regular butter. To make your own, melt unsalted butter over low heat and cook it until it stops bubbling and turns clear—about ½ hour or slightly more. Strain it, leaving behind any solids. You can make this ahead of time and store it in the refrigerator for up to a few weeks.

Coarsely grind the three peppercorns together in a spice grinder of any sort. Sprinkle half, along with ample salt (about 1 teaspoon) on the salmon. No need to pick out bones or remove skin—it will be easier later.

Heat the wine, lemon juice, and 2 sprigs of dill over medium-low heat in a pot with a steamer insert. When the mixture is simmering, add the salmon to the steamer insert. Steam the salmon for about 10 minutes (depending on thickness), until all the meat is opaque.

Remove the salmon and let it cool until you can work with it with your hands. Heat the clarified butter over medium-low heat with the remaining peppercorns.

With your hands, break up the salmon into flakes, removing the skin and bones as you do. Mix the capers and chopped dill in with it. Stuff the salmon mix into a 32-ounce jar or two smaller ones. You can divide it into even more/smaller jars if you want, but you may need to use more clarified butter.

Pour the butter over the salmon and let it settle for a minute, then push the salmon down to make sure that it is fully submerged. Store it in the refrigerator until you're ready to use it.

HALIBUT:
A SILLY LOOKING FISH

Halibut is a silly-looking fish—starting with the fact that it has two eyes on one side of its head. They're born normal—with an eye on each side of the head—but as they lay over, one eye migrates to join the other. So yeah, silly looking and a wee bit creepy. Flat as a pancake, these lovers of chilly waters hang out in the deep sea up and down the West Coast, growing as big as 600 pounds. But the pristinely white fish that you'll find for sale at a fish market likely comes from a smaller fish—20 to 40 pounds of firm flesh. And, as absurd of a creature as they are, they are extremely good for eating.

This was well known by the Native peoples who fished them in the same West Coast waters we do today, using a U- or V-shaped hook made of wood and attached to a rock as a sinker to fish for the bottom-dwelling beasts, sometimes using octopus as bait. The valuable catch was dried or cooked immediately, but either way one fish was enough to feed a village.

Since we rarely are feeding a village, it's nice that—thanks to modern flash-freezing techniques—halibut is available by the fillet at most fish markets. Aside from fillet, during the spring season you may occasionally see halibut cheeks, which are almost more like a large scallop.

When you purchase the fillet, give it a rinse and cook it as soon after defrosting as possible. The key to cooking halibut is recognizing how lean the meat is—unlike a king salmon or black cod, there's no chance of enhancing halibut with the flavors from its natural fats. Instead, embrace both the leanness of the meat and the big flakiness of its texture.

"It's so perfect," says Sena Wheeler of Sena Sea Wild Alaskan Fish. "Don't do anything to it." But she warns that the biggest issue is having it dry out, so it's great with recipes that add plenty of fat—like the Roasted Garlic and Parmesan Baked Halibut on page 70.

In general, halibut isn't valued for its skin, so many recipes (like the Halibut and Asparagus en Papillote on page 73) will leave it off, but it can be great if properly crisped, as on page 83. And of course, don't throw away that skin—take a few extra minutes and turn it into the crunchy treat that is Halibut Chicharrones, on page 87.

ROASTED GARLIC AND PARMESAN BAKED HALIBUT

SERVES 4

Fish, as I note in the Introduction, can be intimidating for those who didn't grow up cooking or eating it. One of the best ways to ease people into eating anything unfamiliar is by smothering it in roasted garlic and cheese. Forget the old Italian maxim of not mixing seafood and cheese: they pair magically and make first forays into cooking and eating halibut easy to execute and even easier to eat.

1 garlic head

½ tablespoon olive oil

1 tablespoon unsalted butter

1 pound halibut, skin removed, in 4 even fillets

Kosher salt, as needed

Freshly ground black pepper, as needed

½ cup mayonnaise

½ cup grated Parmesan

Preheat the oven to 375°F.

Cut off the top of the head of garlic and brush off some of the outer paper skin, leaving just the individually wrapped cloves. On a piece of foil, pour the olive oil over the garlic, then wrap the foil around it and place it in the oven for 45 minutes, until it's completely soft. For the recipe, you'll only need six cloves from the head, but it's worth making a whole head to keep the rest for spreading on crusty bread or adding to salads.

Raise the oven temperature to 425°F.

Heat the butter in an oven-proof pan over low heat. Sprinkle both sides of the fish with salt and pepper. When the butter is melted, add the halibut and put it into the oven for 10 minutes. The fish should be just cooked and opaque throughout.

While the halibut cooks, blend or food process together six cloves of garlic, the mayonnaise, and Parmesan. When the halibut is done, pull it out and generously smear the mayonnaise mixture on the top. Switch the oven to a high broil and return the pan to the still-hot oven for 4 minutes under the broiler, until the top is almost entirely golden brown.

Remove and serve immediately.

HALIBUT AND ASPARAGUS EN PAPILLOTE

SERVES 4

Cooking "en papillote" (in parchment) looks amazing: each diner gets to unwrap their own little package at the table, letting a puff of steam and an enticing smell escape. The process also makes for a gentle way to cook finicky fish, which halibut can be —especially if it was previously frozen. Because halibut is fresh in the spring, it pairs well with the first greens of the season, like slim asparagus and whispers of chives. Any sort of herbs and butter will steam up well in the package, but the complex heat of the piment d'Espelette matches best. If you can't find the spice, substitute a smoky paprika.

4 tablespoons (½ stick) unsalted butter, at room temperature

½ tablespoon piment d'Espelette

1 garlic clove, chopped

½ teaspoon kosher salt

1 bunch asparagus, woody ends removed

1 pound halibut, skin removed, in 4 fillets

1 lemon, in 8 slices

2 teaspoons chopped chives

Preheat the oven to 425°F.

In a food processor, mix the butter, piment d'Esplette, garlic, and salt until they're well incorporated.

Lay out four pieces of parchment paper more than large enough to close over the asparagus and fish. If you don't have parchment, you can use foil.

Chop the asparagus into ½-inch pieces (or even smaller for particularly thick stalks).

Lay down a quarter of the asparagus in the center of the parchment, then place the halibut on top of it, then two slices of lemon. On top, place a pat of the butter (about 1 tablespoon, or a quarter of the total).

recipe continues

Close the parchment by bringing the long edges together and then rolling them together down to the fish. Twist each of the short edges, so it ends up like a candy wrapper. If it's secure, you can just tuck ends under the fish. Alternatively, hold it shut with paper clips. Repeat with the other three packets.

Place all four packets in or on a pan and place it in the oven for about 24 minutes (less for thinner end pieces, more for thicker portions). The parchment should puff up and darken, but not burn.

Plate the fish still in the package and let diners carefully pop them open at the table, then garnish with the chives.

HALIBUT VERACRUZ

SERVES 4

In Mexico's Veracruz state, red snapper pulled from the Gulf takes a dip into an array of Mediterranean ingredients. To add yet another layer of cross-cultural culinary conundrum, here I take the concept and make it using Pacific Northwest halibut. Impressively, the dish uses almost all pantry items rather than fresh and yet still results in a bright, complex flavor—mostly thanks to the olives and capers. Serve it over rice and/or crispy cooked potatoes.

2 tablespoons olive oil

½ teaspoon kosher salt, plus more as needed

Freshly ground black pepper, as needed

1 pound halibut, skin removed, in 4 fillets

1 yellow onion, diced

3 garlic cloves, diced

1 jalapeño, stem and seeds removed, sliced

One 28-ounce can diced tomatoes in puree

½ cup pitted green olives, halved

¼ cup capers

1 bay leaf

½ teaspoon dried Mexican oregano (see note)

Juice of 1 lime

Heat the oil in a large skillet over high heat. Salt and pepper the fish on both sides, then lay the fillets gently in the pan to scar, about a minute on each side—until they release easily from the pan. Remove them from the pan and set aside.

Turn the heat to medium and add the onion and ½ teaspoon of salt, stirring occasionally until the onion begins to caramelize and turn brown, about 7 minutes. Add the garlic and jalapeño slices, cooking until soft, about 3 more minutes.

Add the tomatoes, olives, capers, bay leaf, oregano, and lime juice. Turn the heat back to high and reduce until it is more a thick sauce than a soup mixture, about 6 minutes.

Return the fish fillets to the pan, nestling them down into the sauce, cover, and cook for 2 to 4 more minutes, depending on how thick the fillets are—you can remove the fish and make sure it flakes to check for doneness, or use a thermometer, aiming for 125°F.

If you're having trouble finding Mexican oregano, the best substitute is dried marjoram or dried verbena, but standard oregano will work in a pinch.

AZERI-STYLE HALIBUT SHASHLIK WITH NARSHARAB

SERVES 4

BONNIE MORALES | KACHKA | PORTLAND

Bonnie Morales's Portland restaurant, Kachka, demonstrates how the food of the former Soviet Republics can nestle into the Pacific Northwest, as in this traditional Azerbaijani dish that is typically prepared with sturgeon, but works remarkably well with halibut.

Screaming hot backyard grills have a fraught relationship with fish, leading even many experienced cooks to avoid the combination. But Morales elevates the fish to avoid the pitfall of grill grates grabbing skin: her makeshift mangal (box-like grill) keeps the fish from ever coming into contact with the grill grate, keeping it whole and intact.

"Skewers were never designed to make direct contact with grill grates," Morales explains. "They come from cultures that use things like mangals and robatas. To improvise your own mangal, use paver bricks to suspend skewers across on a grill of your choice. Just know that the grill needs to be rip-roaring hot before you start grilling since the fish does not make contact with the hot grates."

This recipe works best with metal skewers, and Morales strongly suggests V-shaped ones. Without those, it's best to double-thread the fish—onto two parallel skewers—so that you can flip it more easily.

This requires making 6 to 24 hours ahead.

1 tablespoon lightly toasted
 coriander seeds

1 cup European-style sour cream
 (see note)

1 tablespoon Diamond Crystal
 kosher salt (marinade will
 vary wildly with other
 brands or styles), plus more as
 needed

1 pound halibut, skinned,
 deboned, and cut into 2-inch
 pieces

1 garlic clove

1 cup pomegranate juice

¼ cup roughly chopped cilantro

European-style sour cream, or
smetana (Сметана), is actual full-fat
soured cream, unlike many of the
"sour cream" products sold in stores.
Look for it at an Eastern European or
Russian market, or get the Wallaby
brand at Whole Foods. In her book,
Kachka, Morales offers a recipe for it,
or you can search online for a recipe
for smetana.

Grind ½ tablespoon of the coriander seeds in a spice or coffee grinder. Whisk together the sour cream, ground coriander, and salt in a medium bowl. Add the halibut chunks and mix well to evenly coat each piece of fish. Cover the mixture and place it in the refrigerator for at least 6 hours and up to 24 hours.

While the fish is marinating, prepare the narsharab sauce by combining the garlic clove, remaining whole coriander, and pomegranate juice in a saucepan. Bring it to a boil and reduce to a simmer. Continue to simmer until the juice is reduced by half. Strain and discard the solids. Mix in salt to taste. Place the narsharab sauce in the refrigerator until you're ready to cook the skewers.

To cook the fish, heat your grill until it's very hot. While the grill is heating, thread the fish pieces onto the metal skewers. To keep the fish from sticking to the grill grates, place bricks along the front and back of the grill. When grill is hot and ready, balance the skewers with the fish across the bricks and close the lid.

After 4 minutes, check the fish. It should be golden brown with some char. Flip the skewers over. Brush some of the narsharab on the cooked side. When the second side is done, brush narsharab on that side and transfer to a serving platter. Garnish with the cilantro and serve with the remaining narsharab on the side.

HALIBUT SAUSAGE IN CHARD LEAVES

SERVES 4

NICK COFFEY | URSA MINOR | LOPEZ ISLAND

At his Lopez Island restaurant, Nick Coffey keeps things hyperlocal, using ingredients foraged, farmed, and fished almost entirely from the tiny San Juan Island. To make his recipe a bit more accessible to mainlanders, this version uses chard leaves instead of ramp (wild onion), and works fine with instant dashi powder, in case you haven't picked up any seaweed from the beach recently to make your own. The result, no matter the leaf (cabbage works, too, he says), is a subtle, soft fish cake.

When you finish, if you've got more dashi than you need, heat it up with a little soy sauce and mirin, and use it as a broth for the sausage and some noodles. Alternatively, serve the sausage sliced, as an appetizer, with a little dipping sauce made from Japanese (Kewpie) mayonnaise and hot sauce mixed together.

About 5 chard leaves, stems removed

1 pound halibut

1 generous teaspoon kosher salt

¼ cup dashi

Microwave (or lightly steam) the chard for 30 seconds to make it soft and pliable. Let it cool.

Cut the fish into small pieces and remove any skin or bones. Process the fish in a food processor with the salt until very smooth, then add the dashi and process until fully incorporated and sticky.

Place a large piece of plastic wrap on a table and lay out a line of the leaves in alternating directions so they cover a space around 6 inches by 10 inches.

Place the fish puree (enough to wrap up in the leaves to create a cylinder about the diameter of a half dollar) along the middle of the leaves and use the plastic wrap to roll the leaves around the fish. Twist the ends like a candy wrapper. Keep rolling and twisting the plastic wrap to create a tight cylinder.

Cook sous vide at 120°F for 30 minutes or poach in lightly boiling water until the fish is set and an inserted thermometer reaches 120°F (about 20 minutes, depending on the thickness of your roll).

CRISPY-SKIN HALIBUT WITH CREAMED MINTY PEAS AND MOREL MUSHROOMS

SERVES 4

Perfectly cooked fish capped with a layer of audibly crispy skin is, for many, the pinnacle of fish cooking. It can be difficult, intimidating, and extremely frustrating to achieve, if you're not armed with the proper instructions. My goal in this recipe is to put together simple steps and easy-to-follow instructions, which, combined with your trust and patience, will turn out that enviable, shatteringly crisp skin—and a moist, flaky fish beneath.

And once you get that, this recipe pairs it up with two spring favorites—peas and morels. If morels are out of season, you can use pickled or dried (and rehydrated) ones, simply skip them, or use any other type of mushroom, chopped to bite size.

recipe continues

1 pound halibut

2 tablespoons unsalted butter

½ yellow onion, thinly sliced

1 teaspoon kosher salt, plus more
as needed

2 cups fresh or frozen peas

1 tablespoon Champagne
vinegar

¼ pound morel mushrooms

½ cup heavy cream

¼ cup mint leaves

Freshly ground black pepper, as
needed

2 tablespoons vegetable oil

At least an hour before you plan to cook the fish, pull it out of the refrigerator, pat it dry, and then remove any excess moisture from the skin side by dragging the back of your knife over it. If you pat it again with a paper towel, no moisture should remain. Cut the halibut into four portions and return it to the refrigerator, skin side up and uncovered, for 1 hour.

While the halibut dries, prepare the peas and morels. Heat 1½ tablespoons of butter in a large sauté pan over medium heat until melted, then add the onions and 1 teaspoon of salt. Let them cook until soft and just starting to brown, about 5 to 7 minutes.

Add the peas and let them cook until plump but soft, another 5 to 7 minutes. Add the Champagne vinegar to deglaze the pan, using a wooden spoon to get any stuck-on goodness off the pan. Transfer to the blender or to a large cup for use with an immersion blender.

In the same pan (because why clean an extra one?) over medium-high heat, add the remaining ½ tablespoon of butter. When it's melted, add the morels, sprinkle with salt, stir, and then let it sit. Cooking morels is an exercise in patience: the mushrooms will release their water, but then that will evaporate and they will sear up nicely. After about 5 minutes, when the liquid is gone, begin stirring occasionally as they cook another 3 to 4 minutes, until the butter is absorbed and they've caramelized a touch (blackened, starting to stick a bit). Set the mushrooms aside.

Pour the cream into the blender with the pea mixture and add the mint. Blend well, to a puffy, smooth puree.

Remove the fish from the refrigerator and sprinkle generously with salt and pepper. In a stainless steel or well-seasoned cast-iron pan (or anything that is not non-stick), heat 1 tablespoon of oil over high heat until it's smoking. Pour that oil off and heat the second tablespoon of oil until it's very hot, then gently place the fish in, skin side down. Press down gently with a spatula for a few seconds to keep it from curling up. Again, practice patience, leaving it until most of the fish is opaque and the fish lifts easily from the pan, likely about 5 minutes. If you encounter any resistance, leave it a little longer. Flip the fish and let it cook on the non-skin side for barely a minute. Again, it should lift easily. Transfer the fish to a plate to rest for 1 more minute.

Serve the fish skin side up in a puddle of pea puree, sprinkled with morels.

HALIBUT CHICHARRONES

YIELD VARIES

This idea came about as I peeled the skin from my halibut to make another recipe in the book. Fish skin has lots of nutrients, it tastes good when crisped as part of a dish, and here I was about to compost it. Instead, I took inspiration from the Mexican tradition of chicharrones—fried pig skins—and transformed them into a salty snack. This recipe is completely flexible and can be just as easily made with a pile of trimmings from a whole fish as from a few scraps taken off when preparing the Halibut and Asparagus en Papillote (page 73). This also works with salmon skin!

These are great to just snack on, but you can also make them into a nice appetizer with a little crème fraîche and a choice of topping: Pickled Shallots (page 20), salmon roe (see page 46), capers, or a simple snipping of chives.

Halibut skin (as much as you
    have)
Vegetable oil, as needed
Kosher salt, as needed

Dip the skin into boiling water for about 30 seconds. If the skin comes off the fish easily and with very little meat stuck to it, you can even skip this step.

Using the backside (dull edge) of a knife, gently scrape off any lingering bits of meat—you want to make sure that only the skin remains. Don't worry if the skin rips a bit: it will look fine once it's fried. Frying will be easiest if you cut the skin into manageable sections—about 4 inches square or smaller—but if you are a seasoned fryer and have big ambitions, they'll cook fine at any size.

recipe continues

If you have a dehydrator, you can use that to dehydrate the skin. If not, heat an oven to 170°F or whatever its minimum temperature is. Lightly oil as much of a sheet pan as you'll need to lay the skin flat, then spread the skin out, meat side down. Bake the skin until it's dried out and lightly crisp. It should pop off the pan with a little nudge. Depending on skin size and oven temperature, this could take from 30 minutes to 2 hours. Check on it every 20 minutes or so after the first 30.

Heat a ½ inch of oil in a pan to 375°F (if you don't have a thermometer, chip a small piece of the skin and drop it in—it should sizzle up immediately). Set up a rack or paper towel to drain the pieces on. Fry the skin pieces one at a time, as they'll anger the oil and it will bubble and sizzle, then die down again in about 20 seconds. If you want to shape them at all, use tongs to do so as you remove them from the oil. Transfer the skin pieces to the rack or paper towel and sprinkle with salt immediately.

ALBACORE:
NOT JUST
IN CANS

The word "tuna," Sena Wheeler explains, is really no more precise than "fish," as there are so many species of tuna in the ocean. These days, Wheeler focuses her energy on the halibut, black cod, and salmon that her company, Sena Sea Wild Alaskan Fish, fishes for in Alaska, but she got her degree in food sciences working on Oregon Coast albacore.

In other words, don't mistake this for the deep, gem-colored yellow-fin or ahi tuna—you're more likely to see the whitish-rose fleshed albacore canned on the shelf than served at the sushi counter. In fact, those cans are the most common way you'll find albacore, especially outside its late-summer season in the Pacific Northwest. But in season, you can pick up whole or filleted albacore from the docks along the Oregon coast, frozen at Seattle farmers' markets, and in multiple forms at fish markets. More than once I have walked into a fish shop and spotted a beautiful albacore, forgot what I came for, and walked out with an entire fish—the shop broke it down (chef-speak for cut up and portioned) and I walked off with a carcass in one hand (for stock or bait) and a sack of loins ready to use in the other.

Whole, the fish are stunning, streamlined and coming to a sharp point at the mouth, with shimmery, dark-blue skin on top and light, metallic silver lower on the body. The ones I buy whole run around 10 pounds, but they get much bigger.

Once you get the loins home, wipe them off, pat them dry, and store them wrapped in plastic. Know that the meat is extremely soft, so you'll want to be pretty careful with it, especially if you're planning to use it raw (as in the Albacore Crudo on page 98).

If you're cooking it, the meat firms up as it's cooked and will be more solid. In fact, cooked albacore has an intensely meaty texture, but a fairly mild flavor. That means it stands up well to the deep, dark tomato sauce in Jenn Louis's Chreime (page 95), but also flakes easily into Albacore Pasta Salad (page 92).

ALBACORE PASTA SALAD

SERVES 6 TO 8

This pasta salad gives a nice, fresh, local seafood spin on the somewhat stale potluck special. Bright, colorful, and light, it's still hearty enough to last if you make it a day or two ahead.

12 ounces bow-tie pasta (or 4 cups cooked)

1 tablespoon olive oil

Kosher salt, as needed

Freshly ground black pepper, as needed

½ pound albacore loin (or other cut as available)

½ red onion, thinly sliced

1 red bell pepper, chopped

½ cup pitted Kalamata olives, chopped

1 cup chopped parsley

Tomato Dressing (recipe follows)

Cook the pasta per the package directions. Strain the pasta, transfer it to a large bowl, and toss it with ½ tablespoon olive oil. Refrigerate.

Generously salt and pepper the tuna. Heat ½ tablespoon olive oil in a heavy pan over medium-high heat. Sear the tuna for 2 minutes, then roll it to the next side. Repeat until all four sides are seared. Turn off the heat and cover it for about 5 minutes. Transfer it to a cutting board and allow it to cool to room temperature.

Soak the sliced red onion in water for at least 10 minutes.

Chop the tuna into bite-sized pieces. Toss together the tuna, pasta, red pepper, red onion, olives, parsley, and Tomato Dressing, and add salt and pepper to taste.

TOMATO DRESSING

½ tablespoon tomato paste

Juice of 2 lemons

⅓ cup olive oil

¼ teaspoon kosher salt

¼ teaspoon paprika

Meanwhile, make the tomato dressing: Whisk or shake together the tomato paste, lemon juice, olive oil, salt, and paprika until it's completely incorporated.

ALBACORE TACOS

SERVES 4

One of my favorite foods in the world is the cochinita pibil torta at Mexico City's Taqueria el Turix—hardly something that qualifies for this book. But on a recent trip, I learned that the city's Jews substitute tuna for the pork when they make the dish. Using that concept as my inspiration, I incorporate the flavors of underground roasted pork into these tuna tacos.

Start by making the escabeche (recipe follows), letting it marinate while you cook.

Juice of 2 oranges

Juice of 2 limes, plus 1 lime for serving in wedges

½ tablespoon achiote (annatto) paste

1 pound albacore, diced

1 tablespoon vegetable oil

½ red onion, diced

1 teaspoon dried Mexican oregano (see note on page 77)

1 teaspoon kosher salt

⅛ teaspoon cinnamon

Escabeche (recipe follows)

½ bunch cilantro, chopped

8 to 12 corn tortillas, depending on size

Mix the orange juice, lime juice, and achiote paste, making sure to crumble the paste and stir until it's completely dissolved (I've found this is best done with the hands, but will result in your fingers being dyed an orangey-yellow). Add the albacore and marinate it for 30 minutes.

About 10 minutes before the albacore is done marinating, heat the oil over medium heat in a large sauté pan. Cook the diced onion until soft and beginning to brown, about 8 minutes. Add the tuna (drained), oregano, salt, and cinnamon, cooking until just cooked through, about 5 minutes, stirring occasionally.

Serve the escabeche, cilantro, and lime wedges as garnishes, alongside the tortillas to make tacos.

ESCABECHE

1 cup white vinegar

1 habanero, sliced

½ red onion, sliced

Fill a bowl with the white vinegar and 1 cup of water. Add the habanero and sliced red onion and let them marinate for at least 1 hour or as many as 4. Drain them before serving.

CHREIME

SERVES 4

JENN LOUIS

At Ray, her second restaurant, former restaurateur Jenn Louis gathered inspiration from around the Jewish diaspora and brought it to Portland. For this Tunisian Shabbat stew, that means making it with albacore instead of the usual sea bass and using ancho chiles to spike the tomato-based sauce.

While you can serve it with potatoes or rice, as you might any stew, this goes particularly well with olive bread, like a fougasse, to soak up the sauce.

1 pound albacore, in 4 even
    pieces

Juice of ¼ lemon

½ teaspoon kosher salt, plus
    more as needed

Freshly ground black pepper, as
    needed

½ cup olive oil

6 garlic cloves, sliced

3 tablespoons ground ancho
    chile powder (ancho chiles,
    seeds and stems removed,
    whirred in a spice grinder)

One 28-ounce can tomato puree

¼ cup chopped cilantro

Tahini Sauce (recipe follows)

Season the fish with lemon juice and ample salt and pepper in a bowl; set it aside.

Heat the olive oil in a large skillet over medium-high heat. Add the garlic, chile powder, and ½ teaspoon of salt; cook and stir for about 2 minutes. Add the tomato puree and cook, stirring, until slightly darkened, about 5 minutes. Lower the heat if the sauce becomes too thick and add water if necessary to make a relaxed sauce that is neither thick nor watery. Add the fish and cook, covered, until the fish is almost cooked through, about 7 to 9 minutes, depending on the thickness of the fish. Baste the fish with the sauce often. Gently turn the fish over halfway through. Add water a tablespoon at a time as needed to thin sauce if it becomes thick. Salt as needed.

Place the fish on a plate and spoon sauce generously over the top until the fish swims in it. Garnish with the chopped cilantro and a big spoonful of the Tahini Sauce.

recipe continues

TAHINI SAUCE

1 garlic clove

Zest and juice of ½ lemon

½ tablespoon peeled and
chopped ginger

6 tablespoons canola oil

1½ tablespoons tahini

¼ teaspoon kosher salt

Blend the garlic, lemon zest, lemon juice, ginger, and
2 tablespoons of water, until pureed. Add the canola oil, tahini,
and salt, and continue blending until just thickened.

ALBACORE LUNCH BOWL

SERVES 2

Jewel-toned ahi tuna often serves as a centerpiece for elaborate poke bowls at trendy fast-casual restaurants, but its baby brother, the meatier albacore, is what's sustainably caught in our neck of the woods. While its soft flesh doesn't do as well served raw and cubed, this simple lunch dish brings out the best of traditional tuna salad, South American ceviche, and the current poke bowl craze.

1 cup short-grain rice

½ pound albacore

Juice of ½ lime

2 tablespoons mirin

¼ cup Kewpie mayonnaise

2 teaspoons prepared
    horseradish

½ teaspoon kosher salt

2 tablespoons chopped chives

⅓ cup chopped parsley, including
    stems

Cook the rice by your preferred method. While the rice cooks, chop the albacore into approximately 1-inch cubes. Toss the fish with the lime juice and leave it for 20 minutes. Try to time it to finish around when the rice will be ready.

When the rice is ready, add the mirin and fluff with a fork, then split it between two bowls.

Mix the mayonnaise and horseradish together. Add the salt to the fish. Then mix the mayonnaise, fish, chives, and parsley together. Split the fish mixture between the two bowls, dolloping it on top of the rice.

ALBACORE CRUDO

SERVES 4 AS A LIGHT APPETIZER

Crudo, which means "raw" in Italian (and Spanish, in which it is also slang for "hungover"), has come to mean any sort of non-sashimi, raw, sliced fish. This super simple version uses fresh Pacific Northwest albacore for an incredibly fancy-looking but extremely quick pre-meal snack or cocktail party nibble.

4 ounces albacore, sliced thin (see note)

4 pitted Castelvetrano olives, sliced thin

Zest of 1 lemon

2 teaspoons capers

2 teaspoons high-quality olive oil

A hefty pinch of flaky sea salt

Lay the albacore slices out on a plate in a single layer. Scatter the olive pieces, lemon zest, and capers over the top. Drizzle with olive oil and sprinkle with sea salt.

It's totally fine to use frozen albacore here, but instead of completely defrosting it, slice it while it's still pretty frozen, as albacore is a fairly soft fish and that will make slicing thin much easier. If it's fresh, pop it into the freezer for thirty minutes and that will also make it easier.

TUNA NIÇOISE SALAD

SERVES 4

Niçoise salad is as French as it gets: elegant and composed, light but filling, and just the type of thing you want to eat sitting outside while sipping a glass of chilled white wine. But it fits right into the Pacific Northwest, too, with the sweet summer tomatoes blushing into season just as the fresh albacore tuna gets hauled in on the coast. As a bonus, in the hottest part of summer, the few small parts of this recipe that require the stove can be accomplished during the cool morning hours, so that dinner is more assembly than cooking.

This makes a lovely meal as is, but if you have leftovers, pull a few innards out of a loaf of crusty bread and stuff the remaining salad in, then wrap it tightly in plastic or foil, and place it under a weighted pan for 10 to 15 minutes: voila, you now have a second French specialty, *pan bagnat*.

½ cup olive oil

1 pound albacore, in 1-inch cubes

1 pound new potatoes (Yukon Gold or similar), scrubbed

4 eggs

½ pound haricot verts (2 cups), trimmed by removing the ends (the thicker American green beans work as well: just add them to the water a minute earlier)

Niçoise Dressing (recipe follows)

⅛ teaspoon kosher salt, plus more for water

1 cup cherry tomatoes, halved

½ cup Niçoise olives (substitute Kalamata if needed)

4 radishes, thinly sliced

2 scallions, chopped

2 tablespoons capers

Marinate the tuna in ½ cup olive oil for 1 hour. Add both the oil and tuna to a small pan over low heat. Cook the tuna for 10 minutes, until it flakes at the touch. Pull out the tuna and let it cool to room temperature.

Place the potatoes in a large pot of heavily salted water over medium-high heat. When it comes to a boil, gently add the eggs. After 8 minutes, add the haricot verts as well. After 3 more minutes (11 total from the boil), transfer all the contents to a bowl of ice water. When cool, remove everything from the water, and dry. Peel the eggs and quarter.

Use one-quarter of the Niçoise Dressing along with ⅛ teaspoon of salt to dress just the tuna. Arrange the salad by making parallel lines of the beans, tuna, tomatoes, potatoes, olives, and radishes. Put the egg off to one side of the plate.

Top with the additional dressing and garnish with the scallions, capers, and basil.

THE PACIFIC NORTHWEST SEAFOOD COOKBOOK

NIÇOISE DRESSING

20 basil leaves, torn

⅓ cup olive oil

1 garlic clove

4 cured anchovies

¼ teaspoon kosher salt

Juice of 1 lemon

1 tablespoon Dijon mustard

1 shallot, chopped

Prepare the Niçoise Dressing: Mash the garlic, anchovies, and ¼ teaspoon salt together using a mortar and pestle, or chop and then mash them with the flat side of a knife. Move the mixture to a bowl and add the lemon juice, mustard, and shallots. Slowly whisk in ⅓ cup of olive oil.

COD (AND NOT-COD)

Cod has been one of the most important fish—or even foodstuffs—in the world, for much of human history. Mark Kurlansky's eponymous book, *Cod: A Biography of the Fish that Changed the World*, traced it through trade and wars, showing its influence. Pacific cod, specifically caught by the US fleet, which is what we have here—often labeled as "true cod" locally—is generally sustainably fished and is a fairly healthy population, unlike Atlantic cod, which has had a lot of issues over the years with overfishing.

But don't get Pacific cod mixed up with what I like to call the "not-cods": black cod, lingcod, and rockcod or rockfish. These fish, despite the names, are not related to actual cod.

Black cod, also known as sablefish, is sometimes caught incidentally by the halibut fishing industry (with which it shares the spring season), but deserves a spot on the menu in its own right: extremely fatty, it gets a ton of flavor from the oils, which keep the big, soft flakes moist through most any kind of cooking, and helps to caramelize up sauces. "You can't screw it up," says Sena Wheeler. "It's so moist you cannot ruin it, and it has this amazing gourmet taste." She says it's what she makes when she has guests. Though it resembles a goth version of cod, the flavor and texture is very different.

Lingcod, on the other hand, is a hideously ugly fish that looks nothing like cod—its Latin name means "elongated snake tooth." It's not a cod, nor a ling (who names these things?); it's actually a greenling and comes in fantastic colors like bright turquoise. Sometimes you'll even see that show up a bit in the flesh—so if you buy a fillet and notice a bit of blue or blue-green in the white of lingcod, know there's nothing wrong with your fish and the hue will disappear as you cook it. (Old timers, fisherman Amy Grondin says, "rub their hands together in anticipation" when they see the blue flesh, as this is a sign of truly delicious fish.) Lingcod is super plentiful, which makes it a great affordable option for learning to cook fish—and the mild flavor makes it an easy entry point for learning to eat it, too (Grondin says she'll substitute it for halibut, as she prefers the flavor).

Finally, there's rockfish, which isn't even a single kind of fish, but marketing language for the more than 100 varieties that live and act in similar ways. Sometimes you'll see it labeled rockcod, and other times see fun names like cowcod or chilipepper, which are actual species. But again, none are cod. Rather, they belong to a genus of fish collectively known by the science world as Sebastes and by the rest of us most commonly as rockfish. They are a plentiful, easy-to-cook, easy-to-eat kind of whitefish found along the Pacific Northwest coast. Occasionally, you'll see whole rockfish at the fish market, with their eyes bulging from the journey up from the deep water. If you buy it, know that some species have venom in their spines, so use caution or ask your fishmonger to do the work of filleting it for you. Because it can vary by species, there will be a subtle range in flavor and texture, but in general what you'll find on the market are all fairly mild fish, with firm, flaky texture.

Perhaps those inconsistencies make it fitting that it's lumped into a chapter with a bunch of dissimilar fish. If you learn nothing else from this chapter, though, know that a fish having a market name with "cod" in it doesn't necessarily make it like anything else with that in the name.

IPA-BATTERED COD

SERVES 4

Fried fish comes in a million forms, perhaps the best-known around the world being the British fish and chips. To translate that to the Pacific Northwest was easy: the local beer specialty, the IPA, lends itself naturally to food flavors, its bitterness imitating the English beers used across the pond. Also, the chips (fries) got voted off the island: while restaurants have huge boiling vats of oil, allowing them to quickly and easily fry the fish and the fries at the same time, I do not recommend trying this at home. The timing is hard to nail, it requires a ton of oil, and your fries are unlikely to live up to the restaurant version. Roast some broccoli or make some minty peas to go along with this instead. The British would serve this with malt vinegar, Americans with tartar sauce. It's pretty flavorful, but if you're a dipper, have your favorite sauce ready to go.

1 pound cod

⅛ teaspoon kosher salt, plus more as needed

3 cups vegetable oil

¼ cup cornstarch

¼ cup all-purpose flour

⅛ teaspoon cayenne pepper

½ cup Northwest IPA

Remove any skin or bones from the cod (use those tweezers if needed), then slice the fillet horizontally into 2-inch pieces, or your desired size (they'll be fine in any size: I find 2-inch pieces give the best balance of batter to fish). Pat it dry, then sprinkle it with salt and set it aside.

Heat the vegetable oil in a wide pot or high-walled pan over medium-high heat. Ideally, measure for the temperature to get it to about 375°F. Set up a rack or paper towel to drain the fish on after frying.

As the oil heats, prepare your batter. Mix the cornstarch, flour, cayenne, and ⅛ teaspoon of salt together, then stir in the IPA.

Drag each piece of the fish through the batter on its way into the oil, letting the excess drip off and then setting it down into the oil. Fry just a few pieces at a time, so the oil stays hot. If it sinks to the bottom, use a metal spatula to gently nudge it up. After about 60 to 90 seconds, flip the fish over. Fry each piece of fish until it's golden brown on both sides, usually about 2 to 3 minutes total.

Transfer the fish to a rack or paper towel, sprinkling immediately with more salt.

TO GO GLUTEN-FREE

This works really well in a gluten-free version if you just substitute rice flour for the flour and use gluten-free beer. You can use soda water if you don't have gluten-free beer, but go heavy on the salt and cayenne to make up for the loss of flavor.

MARINATED COD TACOS

SERVES 4

KAMALA SAXTON | MARINATION MA KAI | SEATTLE

When Marination Mobile—one of Seattle's most beloved food trucks, serving Hawaiian-Korean tacos—took over a waterfront fish shack on the King County Water Taxi dock and called it Ma Kai (meaning "by the sea"), it worked the same magic on the local cod as it had previously on Spam and Korean beef. Using the brine from pickled jalapeños in the marinade perks up the fish, which, with its Northwest, Japanese, and Mexican ingredients, is the kind of international incident we could all use a lot more of.

Making these cod tacos at home won't live up to eating them from the sunny patio of Marination Ma Kai's West Seattle beachfront, with a window straight from the cocktail bar to the patio and panoramic view of Seattle, but will evoke the same Pacific Northwest beauty.

½ cup sake

3 tablespoons brine from a jar of pickled jalapeños

¾ cup miso paste

3 tablespoons sugar

½ tablespoon kosher salt

3 garlic cloves, smashed with the side of a knife

¼ cup canola oil

1 pound cod, cut into 1-inch strips

Add the sake, brine, miso, sugar, salt, and garlic to a blender or container for use with an immersion blender. Blend the mixture until smooth. Then, with the blender running on slow (if possible), drizzle in the canola oil. Add the oil slowly until it is entirely incorporated and the marinade is emulsified.

Cover the fish in the marinade and let it sit for 30 minutes in the refrigerator.

Heat a large pan over high heat. Lay each piece of cod in the pan. No extra oil should be needed. Cook the fish about 4 minutes on the first side, or until nearly cooked through, then flip for an additional minute or 2—until it lifts easily.

FOR SERVING

8 to 12 corn tortillas

Pickled Shallots (recipe on page 20)

1 cup crema (or sour cream)

½ cup chopped cilantro

¼ cup pickled jalapeño slices

1 lime, sliced

1 tablespoon sesame seeds

Heat the tortillas in the microwave or on a flattop, then serve with the fish, pickled shallots, and all the garnishes, for people to make their own tacos.

BLACK COD KASUZUKE

SERVES 2

SHIRO KASHIBA | SUSHI KASHIBA | SEATTLE

When Shiro Kashiba came to Seattle in 1966, it wasn't yet true that every neighborhood had its own sushi shop—sushi didn't really exist at all in town. The 20-something arrived from training in one of Tokyo's famous sushi houses and pretty much birthed the culinary art here. He taught Seattleites about fish, from tender local geoduck to the Japanese tradition of kasu-marinated fish. Kasu, or sake lees, is what remains behind after making sake. In 1988, the *New York Times* called attention to Kashiba's recipe, naming him the first person in town to serve it at a restaurant. Now, decades later, many local chefs serve it, including the septuagenarian himself, at his latest restaurant, Sushi Kashiba in Pike Place Market. Serve it with warm rice and a little soy sauce.

This requires making 48 hours ahead.

Kosher salt, as needed

Two 5-to-6-ounce black cod steaks, about ¾ to 1 inch thick, sliced at an angle for more meat exposure

Sake, as needed, (optional)

¾ cup sake lees (about ½ pound; see note)

¼ cup white miso paste

1½ cups mirin

2 tablespoons sugar

Cooked rice, for serving

Find sake lees/kasu in the seafood section of a Japanese market

---

Lightly sprinkle the steaks on both sides with salt, then cover and refrigerate them for 24 hours.

After 24 hours, rinse the salt off with the sake or water and pat the steaks dry.

Stir the sake lees, miso, mirin, and sugar together into a paste, to about the consistency of pudding. Slather the marinade on all sides of the steaks, cover, and place them back in the refrigerator. The steaks should be completely covered in the marinade.

After 24 more hours, remove the paste (gently wipe with your finger or a towel). You can stir a little sake into the paste and freeze it for future use. (If you use it a second time, marinate for 48 hours instead of 24.)

Preheat the oven to 450°F on broil. (If you can't set a temperature on your broiler, simply heat the oven to 450°F, then switch to broiler when you put the steaks in.)

Broil the black cod steaks for 8 to 10 minutes. Cooking time will depend on the intensity of your oven, but the fish should blacken on much of the surface and flake at the touch of a fork.

Serve with rice.

MARINATED BLACK COD

SERVES 4

As kids, a dish my brothers and I called "marinated chicken" was a family favorite, and the best part was pouring the leftover sticky-sweet sauce, now imbued with the flavor of the chicken, over white rice. This version, adapted to black cod, uses the same principle: the fish takes on the flavor of the sauce, but also vice versa, meaning the rich fats that make black cod so delectable are now spread throughout the serving of rice.

2 tablespoons soy sauce

½ tablespoon ketchup

¼ cup honey

½ garlic clove, mashed

One 1-pound black cod fillet

Cooked rice, for serving

Preheat the oven to 350°F.

Stir together the soy sauce, ketchup, honey, and garlic.

Pour a bit of the sauce into the bottom of a small roasting dish—just big enough to fit the fish. Add the fish, then pour the rest of the sauce on top. If you don't have a small dish, you may need to double the sauce recipe so it doesn't burn off and char.

Bake for 20 to 25 minutes, depending on the thickness of the fillets (aim for an internal temperature of 130°F, if you're not sure).

Serve with rice and pour sauce from the roasting dish over the fish and rice.

LINGCOD CHAWANMUSHI

SERVES 4 AS AN APPETIZER

Chawanmushi is a Japanese-style custard that uses eggs and dashi to make a silken savory pudding. Aside from being a great way to use up leftover fish bits—this works with nearly any fish or shellfish—it is a relatively simple, quick dish with outsized flavor.

½ pound lingcod

4 teaspoons soy sauce

1 tablespoon mirin

8 dried shiitake mushrooms, rehydrated per package instructions, any stems removed

4 eggs

1½ cups dashi (if you're not familiar with this Japanese stock, I recommend just buying instant)

1 teaspoon fish sauce

1 scallion, chopped

12 sprigs cilantro, chopped

1 teaspoon toasted sesame oil

Remove any skin or bones from the lingcod, then chop it into 1-inch pieces. Mix 1 tablespoon of soy sauce and the mirin together and add the fish. Let it marinate for 30 minutes in the refrigerator. Remove the fish and discard the marinade.

Slice the mushrooms and divide both the mushrooms and the fish among four ramekins or oven-proof ceramic bowls (aim for something that will hold about 12 ounces).

Beat the eggs, then beat in the dashi, 1 teaspoon of soy sauce, and the fish sauce. For the best texture, strain the egg mixture. Then divide the egg mixture, pouring it over the fish and mushrooms. Leave ½-inch of room at the top of the bowl.

In a pot large enough to hold all the ramekins, put in about an inch of water, and let it come to a boil over medium heat. Use foil to cover each of the ramekins, then gently lower them into the pot and lower the heat to medium-low. Cover the pot and let it steam for 15 minutes. You can test these like a cake: poke in a wooden skewer and see if it comes out clean. If so, it's done.

Toss the scallion and cilantro in the sesame oil. Pull the chawanmushi out of the steamer, uncover, add the scallion mixture, and serve.

LINGCOD MUTABBAQ SAMAK

SERVES 4

TAGHREED IBRAHIM

In Iraq, pastry chef Taghreed Ibrahim and her family of five would buy 10 kilograms of fish each week—more than 22 pounds. But when she arrived in the Pacific Northwest as a refugee, she felt lost among the unfamiliar fish. The seafood differed from the river fish she ate back home and she didn't know how to cook what she found here. Her mom used to make this dish, her favorite, at home on weekends, and now she can make it here, using lingcod as a substitute.

1 cup basmati rice

1 teaspoon turmeric

1¼ teaspoons kosher salt

½ cup all-purpose flour

1 teaspoon curry powder

¼ teaspoon freshly ground black
    pepper

1 pound lingcod fillets

1¼ cups vegetable oil

2 medium yellow onions, sliced

¼ cup golden raisins

½ tablespoons ground dried lime
    (see note)

The most important flavor is the dry lime," says Ibrahim. It's worth tracking down at a local Persian or Middle Eastern store or ordering online—you'll sometimes see it called Omani lemon.

Rinse the rice until the water runs clear, then add it to a pot over high heat with 2 cups of water, ½ teaspoon of the turmeric, and ¼ teaspoon of the kosher salt. When it boils, turn the heat down to low and simmer for 20 minutes, then set it aside.

Mix the flour, ½ teaspoon of the salt, curry powder, and black pepper together in a bowl, then add the fish and make sure it gets completely coated.

Heat 1 cup of oil over medium-high heat in a pan big enough to hold all the fish in a single layer. Heat it to at least 375°F (you can test with an edge of fish—it should sizzle upon touching the oil). Set up a rack or paper towel to drain the fish on after frying. Fry the fish for about 3 minutes, then flip and fry 3 more minutes. It should be golden brown on the outside and flake easily if prodded. Let it drain on the rack or paper towel.

Heat ¼ cup of oil over medium-high heat in a medium pan, then add the onions and cook, stirring regularly, until they're golden brown, about 10 to 12 minutes. Add the raisins, ½ teaspoon turmeric, dried lime, and ½ teaspoon of the salt, and stir until well incorporated.

In a medium pot, layer half the rice into the bottom. Add the fish and the onion mix, then a second layer of the rice. Cook over low heat, covered, for 30 minutes.

ONE-PAN ROCKFISH DINNER

SERVES 4

Fish is sort of an introverted food—because of its fragility, it usually cooks best alone. That means making it for a full dinner usually requires a plethora of pans for the various vegetables and starches you'll want on the side. But thick fillets of rockfish can withstand a longer bake in the oven, and in this dish they do just that, making this an easy dinner to set and forget, resulting in something a bit like a dry stew.

1 pound rockfish, in 4 fillets

¼ cup plus 1 tablespoon olive oil

1 teaspoon kosher salt, plus more as needed

Freshly ground black pepper, as needed

1 pound small or new potatoes, cut into halves or quarters to be bite-sized

3 medium tomatoes, quartered

1 medium zucchini, chopped

2 garlic cloves, chopped

2 teaspoons chopped rosemary

2 teaspoons thyme leaves

2 tablespoons chopped parsley

1 lemon, in wedges

Preheat the oven to 400°F.

Rub the fish with 1 tablespoon of the olive oil, salt, and pepper. Put the potatoes, tomatoes, zucchini, and garlic in a bowl and toss with the remaining olive oil, plenty of salt, and pepper. Place them on a baking sheet, then top with the rockfish. Add the rosemary and thyme, then cover with foil and bake for 25 minutes, remove the foil, and bake 10 more minutes.

Remove the sheet from oven, season with additional salt and pepper to taste, and sprinkle with parsley. Serve with the lemon wedges.

TROUT:
THE EVERYMAN FISH

Trout are the everyman fish of the Pacific Northwest. Lakes around the region get stocked by the Department of Fish and Wildlife, making catching them a little like, well, shooting fish in a barrel. Meanwhile, many trout farms—particularly in Idaho, where it's a big industry—grow sustainable, healthy fish without causing harm to the environment. What's more, trout shows up in stores affordably and often.

But before we get too deep into the amazing trout, a little clarification: though it's now stocked and farmed, trout are also native to the Pacific Northwest, including the rainbow trout that we are mostly discussing and cooking here. Cutthroat is very similar and will often be found in the same waters. Steelhead, however, is the name for rainbow trout that migrate to the ocean, which means that while they work in trout recipes, they are often more similar to salmon when it comes to the cooking process—they can be substituted into almost any recipe in which you might use a coho or keta salmon. Not all steelhead are sustainably fished in all parts of the Pacific Northwest, though, so be sure to check into your sourcing. Arctic char, a farmed fish that falls somewhere between steelhead and rainbow, can also be used in those recipes—or in those that call for trout.

Meanwhile, mild, easy to cook, and excellent for stunning guests with whole-fish preparations, rainbow trout make as good a weeknight meal as a dinner party presentation. They don't need to be scaled, and most fishmongers will happily fillet the fish if you'd prefer it off the bone.

Rainbow trout can vary from about 1 pound up to 5, but most that you'll find in stores (and the size we aim for in these recipes) are about 1 pound. Even if you would like them filleted, buy the fish whole, then have your fishmonger fillet it or fillet it yourself. That way, you can have a look at the eyes—the easiest way to check for freshness on whole fish. They should be bright and prominent, not sunken or faded. The skin should all be intact, and, again, bright—it should shimmer. If you touch the fish (or your fishmonger does), its skin should bounce back immediately. Any smell is a sign that it's old.

All farmed trout is considered sustainable, especially in the Northwest where trout farms around the region keep the supply plentiful year-round: Idaho is the country's biggest producer. Why is farming trout sustainable but the same is not true for salmon? There are many reasons, but the biggest difference is that trout are farmed in closed containment systems that separate them from wild fish, while most salmon are farmed in net pens in the ocean where they can come into contact with wild fish. Because these pens are made of netting, there is no way to keep in or out any diseases or pests that are attracted to the stationary fish farm pen. If a pest or disease breaks out in the net pen, the farmer can inoculate the farmed fish, but the wild fish are left to suffer the man-made results on their own. If you wish to learn more, the Monterey Bay Aquarium offers a much more nuanced explanation of the pros and cons of farming fish on their website (seafoodwatch.org).

Once you get the fish home, if you're planning to use it soon, you can leave it as wrapped from your fishmonger. But if you won't get to it that day, pull it from the package, pat it dry, and re-wrap it tightly in plastic. Store it in the coldest section of your refrigerator or over ice (but not in your freezer).

TROUT AMANDINE

SERVES 4

Sometimes the classics are classics for good reason: this recipe is dead simple, but turns out an infinitely elegant dish. The nuttiness of the almonds matches up with hints of the same in the butter, and both cloak the trout without masking its tender texture.

3 tablespoons unsalted butter

⅓ cup slivered almonds

1 whole skin-on rainbow trout, cut into 4 fillets

2 tablespoons all-purpose flour

Kosher salt, as needed

Freshly ground black pepper, as needed

2 tablespoons chopped parsley

½ lemon, in wedges

Melt 1 tablespoon of the butter in a small skillet over medium-low heat. Add the almonds and stir as they cook until brown, about 3 minutes. Remove from the heat.

Melt the remaining 2 tablespoons of butter in a large skillet over medium heat, letting it foam and then darken a bit, about 3 minutes.

Pat the fillets dry and dust both sides with flour, salt, and pepper.

Turn the heat to high and cook the fillets skin side down for about 4 minutes, then flip and cook another 2 to 4 minutes, until they lift easily and are gently colored.

Remove them from the pan, garnish with the almonds and parsley, and serve with a lemon wedge for squeezing over the fish.

TROUT IN SAOR

SERVES 8 AS APPETIZER

In Italy, this sour topping traditionally goes on sardines, where the vinegar-based marinade came about as a method of preservation for fishermen, with the raisins added for sweetness. But here in the Pacific Northwest, the big flavors complement the mildness of trout. As with all the trout recipes, it works for the ubiquitous farmed rainbow trout, but I particularly love this for the middle cousins of the trout-to-salmon spectrum—Arctic char and steelhead trout—because of their color and because their heartiness stands up well to the flavors.

Once ready, you can either eat the fish alone, in the chunks, or flake it up, mix it with the onions, and serve it on crackers.

This requires making 24 hours ahead.

¼ cup raisins

1 cup dry white wine

4 tablespoons extra virgin olive oil

1 red onion, thinly sliced

1 cup apple cider vinegar, plus more as needed

1 teaspoon sugar

2 tablespoons pine nuts

Zest of 1 lemon

½ teaspoon kosher salt, plus more as needed

Freshly ground black pepper, as needed

1 pound steelhead or Arctic char, cut into 2-inch chunks

1 tablespoon chopped parsley

Soak the raisins in the wine.

Heat 2 tablespoons of the olive oil over medium heat and cook the onion until it's just soft, about 15 minutes.

Stir in the raisins and wine mixture, vinegar, sugar, pine nuts, and lemon zest. Season with salt and pepper to taste. Let it come to a boil and burn off the alcohol, just 2 minutes or so—don't let it go too long as the liquid will start to reduce. You can remove this mixture from the pan and set it aside, then wipe out the pan to use it for the fish.

Season the fish on both sides with salt and pepper.

Heat 2 tablespoons of the olive oil over high heat and sear the fish for 2 minutes skin side down. Flip it and sear an additional minute. Transfer to a dish or jar large enough to fit the fish and small enough to keep them submerged under the onions and liquid, which you should add on top.

Make sure the fish is completely covered—add extra vinegar if needed. Cover the dish or jar and refrigerate for at least 24 hours and up to 48. Bring the fish back to room temperature before serving, and garnish with the parsley.

CHINESE-INSPIRED WHOLE TROUT

SERVES 4

"No!" my friend Nick yelled. I'll never forget the look on his face when I tried to flip over the fish to get to the meat underneath at a restaurant in Beijing. I was about to make a major faux pas and earn us all bad luck. "You'd flip the boat that we're all in," he explained.

Now, I think about that every time I eat whole fish—which is pretty often, especially when armed with this absurdly easy Chinese-inspired version.

To serve the fish whole, gently insert a butter knife parallel to the fish, just above the spine. The whole fillet will jump easily right off the bone. Once you've plated that, wiggle the head a touch and pull up, like you're removing a Band-aid, and the whole skeleton will come right out—leaving the bottom meat ready for eating and keeping the boat that we're all in upright and speeding ahead toward a lovely dinner. Serve over white rice and be generous when pouring the sauce over the top.

1 whole rainbow trout, ideally about 1 pound, cleaned and gutted

Kosher salt, as needed

4 scallions

1 inch ginger, julienned

3 garlic cloves, sliced

Soy Sauce Dressing (recipe follows)

Cooked rice, for serving

Rinse off the fish and pat it dry, then salt it heavily inside and out and let it rest for 30 minutes.

Chop 3 scallions and slice the fourth into long shreds. To keep that one fresh, set it in cold water until the cooking is finished.

Wipe off the fish and pat it dry, then arrange it on any heatproof plate. Mix together half of the ginger, chopped scallions, and garlic, and put half inside the fish and the other half on top.

Heat a small amount of water over medium heat in a wok or large pot in which your steamer or a plate fits. When it starts to boil, place the plate with the fish on it either into the steamer, or put a few balls of foil into the pot and lower the plate onto that, making sure it stays above the water. Cover and cook for 12 minutes (more for a larger fish, less for a smaller one).

When it's nearly done, make sure your dressing (below) is hot and ready. Remove the fish at the end of 12 minutes, pour the dressing over the top and garnish with the sliced scallions.

SOY SAUCE DRESSING

1 inch ginger, chopped

1 garlic clove

½ cup soy sauce

2 tablespoons Shaoxing wine
    (this is a Chinese cooking
    wine, but a dry sherry would
    make a fine substitute if
    needed)

1 tablespoon toasted sesame oil

1 teaspoon honey

Mix all the ingredients together in a small saucepan and bring it to a simmer for at least 2 minutes or as long as 10.

TROUT WITH SPRING PEA SALSA VERDE

SERVES 4

WILL GORDON | WESTWARD | SEATTLE

Westward's spot on the shore of Lake Union in Seattle could let it rest on its view alone to attract business, but instead it relies on its wood-fired oven to turn out impressive Mediterranean-style, Northwest seafood dishes. The whole-roasted trout is a perennial favorite, and this version has a few adjustments to allow home chefs to cook it in their own oven. Too bad you can't recreate the Adirondack chairs and oyster-shell beachside firepit, too.

Trout is one of the easiest fish to cook whole, and its impressive looks belie the relatively little work needed to make it. Laid on top of the bright green puree and covered in the cascade of spring vegetables, it's perfect for showing off at a dinner party—and it's easy and affordable to double if it's a big party.

2 cups fresh peas

2 cups snap peas, cut diagonally

¾ cup olive oil

¼ cup slivered almonds

Kosher salt, as needed

½ small bunch parsley (about
   1 cup)

2 tablespoons brined capers

2 garlic cloves

3 cured anchovies (about
   ½ tablespoon tightly packed)

1 tablespoon basil

Preheat the oven to 450°F.

Blanch the peas and snap peas, separately, in boiling water for about 90 seconds each, then transfer them to a bowl of ice water. Set them aside until ready to use.

Heat 1 tablespoon of olive oil in a small pan over medium heat and toast the almonds with a pinch of kosher salt, about 3 to 4 minutes, until just fragrant. Set them aside.

Blend the parsley, peas, capers, garlic, anchovies, basil, the zest of ½ lime (save this ½ lime for juicing into the salad), and ½ cup olive oil until very smooth, then taste it and salt accordingly (about 1 teaspoon). Chill the mixture in the refrigerator until ready to use.

recipe continues

1 lime, peeled with a knife and chopped, plus zest and juice of ½ lime

2 tablespoons vegetable oil

1 whole rainbow trout, ideally about 1 pound, cleaned and gutted

¼ cup mint leaves (tear any larger ones, leave smaller ones whole)

¼ cup Pickled Shallots (page 20)

½ cup pea shoots (optional, as these will be hard to find out of season)

Sea salt flakes, as needed

In a large, oven-safe cast-iron or sauté pan, warm the vegetable oil over high heat and sear the trout until the skin is crisped on the first side, about 3 to 4 minutes. Flip the fish, carefully pour out the oil, then place the entire pan in the oven for 10 minutes until the fish is cooked through (if taking a temperature, look for 135°F).

While the trout cooks, spoon the parsley mixture onto a platter.

When the fish is done, plate it on top of the puree.

Mix all the salad ingredients together: the snap peas, mint leaves, almonds, the chopped lime, the juice of the zested lime, 3 tablespoons olive oil, and the pickled shallots. Top the fish with the salad, add the pea shoots (if using), and drizzle any leftover juices from the salad over the fish. Sprinkle with salt flakes.

Bring it to the table as-is to show off the dish, and then you can either parcel out the fillets—just as in the Chinese-Inspired Whole Trout on page 122—or let people grab at the fish with their forks along with the salad and puree. Start with the fork at the spine and pull down toward the belly to minimize bones coming off with the meat.

SHEL

CRAB:
THE LOBSTER
OF THE WEST

While salmon might be the diva of Pacific Northwest seafood, Dungeness crab is the ingénue who steals the show. The habitat of this big, purple crab stretches from San Francisco up to Alaska, but the heart of Dungeness country is on the Olympic Peninsula of Washington, where their eponymous spit of land juts into Puget Sound.

Dungies, as they're sometimes called, give sweet, soft meat, more comparable to a lobster from Maine than to its East Coast crab brethren. Like lobster, the best, most pure expression of Dungeness flavor involves eating them nearly unadulterated: fresh, cooked, and cracked, and just maybe dipped in butter. But that doesn't mean they don't do wonders for any number of other dishes: Dungeness Crab and Baby Beet Salad (page 144), Dungeness Mac and Cheese (page 146), and Dungeness Crab Deviled Eggs (page 138) among them.

And though Dungeness are available basically year-round in the Pacific Northwest, the recreational fishing seasons vary just a bit, leading crab to be very much a summer favorite for us in Seattle.

On warm July and August days, we'll take a few folding chairs down to a dock and toss in our ring traps loaded with anything from salmon carcasses to cat food, pulling them up every half-hour or so to check for crabs. Though it's not the most efficient way to crab, it turns an otherwise passive activity into a suspense-filled adventure. Plus, there are magazines to read and snacks to eat in between. Sometimes we'll catch the limit of six Dungeness; other times we'll come home with only a few consolation-prize red rock crab—they're smaller and slightly less sweet, but will do in a pinch.

Most people who go crabbing around here do it by lowering a box trap from a boat and leaving it there for the day. It is far more efficient, but not nearly as efficient as my method of ensuring that, no matter what, my day of crabbing ends with a feast: stopping at a local market to pick up live crab on the way home. It's still cheaper than owning a boat!

Catching Dungeness from the pier or a boat means checking to make sure they're male and big enough to take home (female and small crabs must be thrown back)—when you purchase your crabbing license you'll also receive the rules that spell out how to know if a crab is a "keeper" or needs to be released. Buying them at the market lets me make sure they have all their legs and are feisty—you always want to buy fighters. Once you get them home, you'll want to cook them as soon as possible.

The easiest way—and the traditional manner—is to simply steam or boil them whole in a pot, about 14 minutes for steaming and 10 for boiling for the average 2-pound crab. The most humane and even way to cook crab is to kill them first and then steam them, as per the instructions on page 133.

While doing that, you can save the crab fat—the innards, really—to make the incredible Filipino dish, Aligue Rice with Tomato Salad, on page 150. Once they're steamed, you can use the legs in Cioppino (page 222) or eat them with Lemon Drawn Butter (page 137), or pull out the crabmeat and make any of the other dishes in this book.

You can also buy either a cooked crab or Dungeness crabmeat at the store—the latter being extremely helpful if you're not patient or coordinated enough to get all those little pieces of crab out. When extracting the meat yourself, the usual rule of thumb is that you'll find about a quarter of the crab's weight is meat. I tend to look for about 2- to 2½-pound crabs, which gives me 8 to 10 ounces of meat, a helpful calculation if you're buying whole crabs with the intention of using them for the recipes here (none of which, I should add, will suffer from an approximation, should your crab not live up to these size expectations or overwhelm them). When buying Dungeness meat, the main thing is to make sure it looks damp and healthy—neither dried out nor sitting in water—and smells like something you would want to eat.

HOW TO KILL AND CLEAN A LIVE CRAB

Place the crab in a freezer for about 20 minutes to slow its movements.

Hold the live crab by its back two legs. If you look on the belly (the underside), you'll see a triangular pattern that points about three-quarters of the way up the belly from the back. The tip of that is the nerve center. To kill a crab humanely before cooking, you need to crush that. You can do it with a knife, if you're confident in your knife skills, but the narrowness and hard shell make that quite difficult.

The easier method (not that easy) is to hold it by two of the back legs on each side and aim that tip to the corner of a counter. Hold the crab and gently touch the spot you're trying to hit on the corner once or twice gently to get your aim correct, and then slam that spot on the crab quickly and with force—as if swinging for a home run. It seems violent, but a single, swift blow is, in fact, the most humane way to do this.

After a strong hit, your crab should stop moving and will start leaking water—move it directly to the sink. Hold all the claws from each side and twist in opposite directions. One side will come off, then repeat with the second side to remove it from the shell. If you're making the Aligue Rice with Tomato Salad (page 150), make sure to save the innards (all of the orange and related goo) that are sitting in the top shell, then discard the shell (or wash and save to use as part of a nice presentation of a dish). Wipe any innards from the leg halves.

You'll see spiky, off-white pieces on top of the remaining body, with a sort of corduroy feel. Those are the gills; remove them. Your final crab halves should be all shell and translucent or white meat. Now you have cleaned crab halves, ready to use!

Follow the instructions on page 137 to steam the meat.

HOW TO PICK A CRAB

Once you've cooked the crab, you need to get at that tasty meat. For recipes like the Dungeness Crab Deviled Eggs (page 138) and Dungeness Crab Pasta (page 141), you'll need to do it yourself. If you're serving steamed halves, like on page 137, just put out the implements and let your guests go to town.

More skilled seamen than I like to "shake" a crab: gently crack it a bit and then quite literally shake it over a bowl. Despite repeated lessons, this has always resulted in the few bits of crab that come out landing all over my kitchen and more shell than meat in the bowl, so I prefer the traditional crack-and-pick method.

Crab crackers, the tool supposedly designed for cracking crab, also tend to actually work less well for the task than a wooden rolling pin or the smooth side of a metal meat tenderizer.

Start by separating the body from the legs. To get the meat from the body (that is, all the non-leg parts), gently tap with your tool a few times, then use your fingers to pull off chunks and your fingers or a chopstick to dig out the chunks of meat from the honeycomb-like maze of soft shell.

For each of the legs and claw, lay it across the cutting board, then stand it up on edge, so that you can hit each segment longitudinally, rather than on the flat sides. Use your tool to give a quick, sharp rap or two on each segment, cracking it and bouncing your tool up, rather than squishing the shell down into the meat (the way a cracker does). Start from the small end of the leg—pull off the last pointy segment and use it to help pull the meat from the other segments. Repeat with all the limbs.

If you're picking it for a dish, double- or even triple-check your meat to make sure you don't have any shell bits left. You will, it always happens. Check it as methodically and carefully as you can, and then check again as you put it into the dish.

STEAMED DUNGENESS CRAB WITH LEMON DRAWN BUTTER

SERVES 4

Steamed Dungeness crab is the summer special of the Pacific Northwest, best when it's fresh caught from Puget Sound and eaten over newspaper while the summer sun hangs late in the sky. The meat, sweet with the saltwater, requires almost no flavoring, but a little lemon drawn butter is nice to have—if for nothing else, then as a dip for a side dish of thick, crusty bread. While some of the other recipes in this book work fine with crab bought already cooked and killed or with lump crabmeat, I recommend starting this with a live crab for the best flavor.

2 large Dungeness crabs, killed and cleaned (instructions on page 133)

Kosher salt, as needed

4 tablespoons (½ stick) unsalted butter

Juice of ½ lemon

Steam the four halves of crab over a medium boil of heavily salted water for about 14 minutes (assuming approximately 2-pound crabs: add a minute for each additional half-pound per crab).

Transfer the steamed crabs to a bowl of ice water to cool for 5 minutes.

To make the lemon drawn butter, heat the butter over medium-low heat for about 5 minutes, skimming the foam off the top with a spoon. Remove the butter from the heat and pour it into a bowl, leaving behind the milk solids collected at the bottom. Stir in the lemon juice.

DUNGENESS CRAB DEVILED EGGS

MAKES 16 DEVILED EGG HALVES

The silky sweetness of cooked Dungeness crab adds texture and flavor to this classic appetizer. You can simplify this by skipping the step of reserving the chives and crab, but if you're bringing this to a party (they'll go fast) or making it to impress guests, it shows off the star ingredient. If you end up with extra filling, consider it a cook's snack and spread it on a cracker or use it as a dip with potato chips.

8 eggs

4 to 5 ounces cooked Dungeness crabmeat (from about ½ crab)

2 tablespoons chopped chives

2 tablespoons mayonnaise

1 tablespoon Dijon mustard

1 teaspoon apple cider vinegar

Juice of ¼ lemon

½ teaspoon kosher salt

Freshly ground black pepper, as needed

Paprika, for sprinkling

Cayenne pepper, for sprinkling (optional)

Bring a pot of water to a boil over medium heat and gently lower in the eggs. Boil for 10 minutes, then transfer to a bowl of ice water for 5 minutes.

Peel the eggs and slice them in half lengthwise. Remove the yolks and place them in a bowl. If you don't have an egg plate to rest the white halves, crinkle up some foil, then unfold. The resulting nooks and crannies will hold the eggs.

Reserve 16 large-ish clumps of crab and about a teaspoon of chopped chives.

In a bowl, mash together the yolks, mayonnaise, mustard, remaining chives, vinegar, and lemon juice. When the mixture is mostly smooth, add the remaining crabmeat, salt, and pepper and stir gently. Taste and adjust any seasonings.

Cut a half-inch slit in the corner of a zip-top bag and fill the bag with the yolk-mayonnaise mixture. Gently squeezing the bag, use it to fill the cavity of each egg white generously with the mixture, mounding it up over the top.

Once all eggs are filled, top each egg with a piece of the reserved crab. Sprinkle the reserved chives over the top, then dust the eggs with paprika, and, if you like heat, a bit of cayenne pepper.

CRAB ESQUITES

SERVES 6 TO 8 AS A SNACK

Around Mexico, street-side stands serve steaming Styrofoam cups full of esquites, or corn-off-the-cob. Loaded with mayo, cheese, and a gentle kick of chile powder, they are a bit sweet, a bit spicy, and plenty comforting. In this version, corn's best friend—crabmeat—joins the party and melts right in, giving it a hint of fanciness that takes it from the street to the party. Serve it in small bowls with a spoon at the table, or in a big bowl alongside tortilla chips at a picnic.

4 ears corn

4 tablespoons (½ stick) unsalted butter

4 to 5 ounces cooked Dungeness crabmeat (about ½ crab)

¼ teaspoon kosher salt

¼ cup mayonnaise

½ cup queso fresco (or similar crumbly cheese)

Chile powder, as needed

1 lime, sliced into wedges

Husk the corn and place it into heavily salted boiling water for about 5 minutes. Remove it from the water and allow it to cool enough to slice the kernels off with a knife.

Heat the butter in a large pan over medium heat. When melted, add the corn kernels and cook them for about 2 minutes, just long enough to meld well with the butter and heat through. Remove the pan from the heat and stir in the crab, the ¼ teaspoon salt, and mayonnaise.

Place the mixture in the final serving vessel and sprinkle queso fresco over the surface. Dust with chile powder and any additional salt, as needed. Serve with lime wedges for squeezing over the corn.

DUNGENESS CRAB PASTA

SERVES 4

BRIAN CLEVENGER | GENERAL HARVEST RESTAURANTS | SEATTLE

So you finish up your crab dinner and have a few lumps left over . . . or maybe your crabbing excursion came up a little short: no problem. This recipe takes a tidbit of crab and extends it through a bowl of pasta as if you were shoveling lumps of meat into your mouth with every bite.

While Brian Clevenger specializes in making near-perfect pasta, I don't recommend making your own noodles if you don't have a pasta roller—it's a lot of work and stores sell perfectly good fresh pasta. But if you either have a pasta machine or feel like taking on a project, these silky-textured, rich noodles make great company for the crab.

The fresh pasta recipe here makes about twice as much as you'll need for the recipe—you can freeze the other half and cook it straight from the freezer the next time you want a quick treat.

If you're buying store-bought fresh pasta, get about 4 ounces per person.

2 tablespoons unsalted butter

1 fennel bulb, diced

4 servings Fresh Noodles (half of the recipe that follows)

6 ounces cooked Dungeness crabmeat

Zest and juice of 2 lemons

2 tablespoons crème fraîche

2 tablespoons chives, snipped

Kosher salt, as needed

Freshly ground black pepper, as needed

Boil heavily salted water in a large pot.

Heat the butter in a large pan over medium heat. Once it melts, sauté the diced fennel until it just begins to color, about 3 minutes.

Add the pasta to the salted water and cook for 2 minutes (or a few minutes longer if using store-bought pasta—you want it just short of al dente). Reserve ¼ cup of the pasta water.

Add the noodles and reserved pasta water to the fennel pan and cook another 2 minutes on high heat.

Stir in the crab, lemon zest, crème fraîche, and chives. Remove the pan from the heat and season it with the salt, pepper, and lemon juice.

recipe continues

FRESH NOODLES

2 cups semolina flour

1 cup all-purpose flour, plus more
for dusting

½ tablespoon kosher salt

4 egg yolks

1 whole egg

1½ tablespoons extra virgin
olive oil

¼–½ cup warm water

Put the two flours and the salt in the bowl of a stand mixer (or any large bowl if you're making the pasta by hand), then separately mix together the egg yolks, whole egg, olive oil, and ¼ cup of warm water in another bowl.

Using the dough hook on low speed, combine the dry ingredients (or by hand, if you're not using a mixer). Slowly add in the egg mixture. Add more warm water as needed, up to another ¼ cup, until the dough begins to form (kneading, if by hand).

Transfer the dough from the bowl to a well-floured surface and, using your palms, fold the dough over itself, repeating until a tight ball forms, about 6 to 8 minutes.

Wrap the dough in plastic and let it rest at least 30 minutes before rolling.

Roll out the dough as thin as possible in a pasta machine, likely in 6 to 8 sheets, dusting with flour as necessary to prevent sticking. Then cut the noodles to a little over ¼ inch wide. Hang them to dry on a chair back or laundry rack as you finish cutting.

PNW CRAB CAKES WITH CHIVE AIOLI

SERVES 4 AS AN APPETIZER, 2 AS AN ENTRÉE

Simple, classic, and weirdly elegant, crab cakes are the most typical way to use fresh-picked crab. This recipe stays pretty true to tradition, but leave the Old Bay at home: this ain't Maryland. The mustard provides plenty of flavor—as does the crab itself, thanks to the sweetness of Dungeness. By making these a little on the miniature side, they will hold together better and crisp up nicely when fried in butter.

½ pound cooked Dungeness crabmeat (from approximately 1 crab)

1 egg, lightly beaten

1 cup breadcrumbs

1 teaspoon Worcestershire sauce

3 scallions, thinly sliced

1 tablespoon stone ground mustard

1 tablespoon unsalted butter

1 lemon, in wedges

Chive Aioli (recipe follows)

To make the cakes, mix the crab, egg, ¾ cup of the breadcrumbs, Worcestershire sauce, scallions, and mustard. Form the mixture into golf ball–sized circles, then flatten them a bit, to about ¾ inch thick. Spread the remaining breadcrumbs on a plate and dip both sides of each cake into them for an extra coating. Refrigerate the cakes for 10 to 20 minutes. Make the Chive Aioli as they chill.

To cook the cakes, heat the butter over medium-high heat. Place the cakes in the butter and cook until they are golden brown and crispy, about 2 minutes. Flip and repeat on the second side, another 2 minutes. If you have a smaller pan, you may want to do this in two batches, adding a little extra butter for the second batch.

Serve with the Chive Aioli dolloped on top.

CHIVE AIOLI

¼ cup mayonnaise

1 tablespoon chopped chives

2 garlic cloves, mashed

Mix the mayonnaise, chives, and garlic together.

DUNGENESS CRAB AND BABY BEET SALAD

SERVES 4

ETHAN STOWELL | ETHAN STOWELL RESTAURANTS | SEATTLE

Ethan Stowell grew his restaurant empire on interpreting the ingredients of the Pacific Northwest through different seasons and styles, and he is often at his best when showcasing the region's seafood—as in this salad. Hefty with piles of crab, it's happy to pretend to be a starter but plentiful enough for a full dinner; to pretend to be spring with its baby beets and watercress, but taste like the bright sun of summer. Stowell advises you to enjoy this with a nice glass of rosé.

12 baby beets, peeled and quartered (if you can't find baby beets, chop up about 5 regular beets; they won't be as tender, but will work)

2 tablespoons vegetable oil

1 teaspoon kosher salt, plus more as needed

Juice of 2 lemons

Juice and zest of 1 orange

2 tablespoons extra virgin olive oil, plus more as needed

Freshly ground black pepper, as needed

Preheat the oven to 425°F.

Rub the baby beets with the vegetable oil and a teaspoon of salt, and roast them for 20 minutes or until they are soft. Let them cool.

Marinate the roasted beets in the juice of 1 lemon, zest of the orange, olive oil, and black pepper, for around 20 minutes.

Split, pit, and chop the avocado, then puree it in a food processor until it's smooth. Add lemon juice and salt to taste, likely about a ½-lemon of juice. If it's more paste than puree texture, thin a bit more with water, lemon juice, or a mix. It should be thick, but not immobile.

1 large avocado

12 ounces cooked Dungeness
crabmeat

1 bunch watercress, cleaned

4 red radishes, shaved paper-thin

Divide the avocado puree among four plates, then top it with the beets. Pile the Dungeness crab on top, then sprinkle with the watercress and radish slices. Drizzle with a small amount of olive oil, the juice of the remaining half-lemon, and a little juice from the orange.

DUNGENESS MAC AND CHEESE

SERVES 8

JASON ALDOUS | FRIDAY HARBOR HOUSE | SAN JUAN ISLAND

Dungeness crab does wonders for macaroni and cheese, nestling into all the nooks and crannies of the pasta and complementing the richness of the cheese. Overlooking Friday Harbor, Jason Aldous's restaurant, Friday Harbor House, serves this fried into little balls and topped with pickled bull kelp. While few readers will be heading out to collect the seaweed to start that recipe, the bread and butter pickles sprinkled on top give this a great pop. And if you do have any leftovers, don't hesitate to scoop them out, sprinkle on some breadcrumbs, and give it a little fry.

3 tablespoons unsalted butter

½ large sweet onion, minced

1 fennel bulb, minced

4 garlic cloves, minced

1 pound macaroni

2 tablespoons all-purpose flour

1½ cups heavy cream

1 bay leaf

4 ounces IPA beer

Zest of 1 lemon

1 tablespoon stone ground mustard

¼ teaspoon cayenne pepper

½ teaspoon smoked paprika

1 teaspoon kosher salt

Heat 1 tablespoon of the butter in a small pan over medium-high heat and sauté the onion, fennel, and garlic for 3 to 4 minutes. Set them aside.

Cook the macaroni in salted water. While that cooks, you can begin making the sauce. When the noodles are al dente, drain and set them aside until the cheese sauce is ready.

Heat the remaining 2 tablespoons of butter in a large pot over medium heat until it's just beginning to brown, about 3 minutes. Add the flour, and cook for 5 more minutes, stirring, to make a roux. Add the cream, bay leaf, beer, lemon zest, mustard, cayenne, paprika, and salt, and turn to low heat. Cover the mixture and let it infuse for about 10 minutes.

½ cup shredded smoked
   mozzarella (about 4 ounces)
1½ cups shredded Gruyère (about
   7 ounces)
¼ cup shredded Parmesan (about
   1 ounce)
1½ cups shredded white Cheddar
   (about 7 ounces)
½ pound cooked Dungeness
   crabmeat
1 cup bread and butter pickles

On the cheeses, I've given
approximate weights in to help guide
you in your shopping, but you can
use the cup measurements to cook.

Turn off heat and stir in the cheeses until they're completely
combined. Add the onion and fennel mixture, macaroni, and
crab. Top with the pickles and serve.

CRAB MOFONGO

SERVES 4

ERIC RIVERA | ADDO | SEATTLE

Eric Rivera is something of a culinary chameleon: he's touched the top tier in his time at Chicago's renowned Alinea but also helped develop one of Seattle's best burgers at Great State Burger. His Addo incubator provides a platform to some of Seattle's best up-and-coming chefs, and he runs a few of his own restaurant concepts out of the space, including Lechoncito, which serves food from Rivera's Puerto Rican background. This dish pinpoints the sweet spot of his heritage and hometown—Olympia, Washington—bringing Dungeness crab into this traditional Puerto Rican mashed plantain dish.

4 green (unripe) plantains

1 red bell pepper

1 green bell pepper

1 Spanish onion

6 garlic cloves

4 ounces bacon

4 ounces cooked Dungeness
   crabmeat (about ½ crab)

Sazon (recipe follows)

1 lime

Peel and cut the plantains into 1-inch medallions. Cut the red bell pepper, green bell pepper, and onion into ½-inch squares, and roughly chop the garlic.

Render the bacon over medium-high heat in a large pan until it's crispy, about 6 to 8 minutes, then remove the bacon from the pan and chop it. Add the plantains to the fat, turning occasionally, cooking until the color starts to turn gold on all sides. Remove them before they start to darken to black or brown, likely about 5 to 8 minutes.

Add the onion, red bell pepper, green bell pepper, and garlic and cook until the onion turns translucent, about 5 to 7 minutes.

Place half of each of the cooked plantains, bacon, crab, and vegetables, plus 1 teaspoon of Sazon into a pilon (similar to a mortar and pestle) and mash. If you don't have a pilon, you can also use a sturdy potato masher. Squeeze half a lime over it. It should be soft and well mashed—you can form it into a ball or mold it into a bowl for serving (if it's not soft enough, add a little water or stock as you mash). Add the rest of the plantains, bacon, crab, and vegetables, another teaspoon of Sazon, and mash a little more. Season with the other half of the lime. Taste and add more Sazon if necessary.

SAZON

1 tablespoon achiote (annatto)
    seed
2 teaspoons cumin seed
1 teaspoon yellow mustard seed
1 teaspoon black peppercorns
½ teaspoon coriander seed
½ tablespoon turmeric
4 tablespoons kosher salt
½ teaspoon MSG
1 tablespoon oregano
1 tablespoon Spanish paprika

Toast the achiote seeds, cumin, mustard, black peppercorns, and coriander for about 3 minutes in a dry pan, until they're fragrant. Grind them well and mix with the remaining ingredients.

ALIGUE RICE WITH TOMATO SALAD

SERVES 6

AARON VERZOSA | ARCHIPELAGO | SEATTLE

Aligue rice, explains Aaron Verzosa, is a common dish in the Philippines that uses the fat from crabs to flavor rice. But he grew up eating it after crabbing with his family on the Oregon coast. He reminisces: "In its simplest form, making this dish came from snatching a Dungeness crab head before anyone noticed, and using it as a bowl to mix a couple of heaping scoops of hot rice into the fat." This version is a bit more complicated, but, like his memory, bridges growing up in the Pacific Northwest and his family's roots in the Philippines.

If you're making steamed crabs and want to do something cool with the insides—which are all too often tossed out—this dish makes for good eating along with the crabmeat.

6 cups cooked rice (about 3 cups uncooked)

½ cup vegetable oil

24 shallots, diced (see notes)

¼ cup minced garlic (almost 1 small head)

2 tablespoons kosher salt

2 tablespoons unsalted butter

3 tablespoons pickled hot peppers (like Mama Lil's), minced

Fat from 1 Dungeness crab (see notes)

2½ tablespoons finely chopped chives

Tomato Salad (recipe follows)

Have the cooked rice ready to go or timed to finish as soon as you start to cook the rest of the recipe.

Heat the vegetable oil in a large pan over medium heat. Sweat the shallots until they are softened, about 5 minutes. Add the garlic and 1 tablespoon of salt and cook to a light golden brown, about 4 more minutes. Add the butter and peppers and cook the whole thing until they are nicely caramelized. Stir in the crab fat and juices and the remaining tablespoon of salt. It may seem salty, but it will be seasoning the whole batch of rice.

Turn off the heat and fold in the hot rice. Mix in the chives. Taste for seasoning, then serve with the Tomato Salad on the side—or on top, as it makes the perfect foil for the rich rice.

For the shallots, I highly recommend using a food processer and pulsing to dice. Kill the crab as described on page 133. Scrape out and use all the orange innards and liquid from the shell; you will have about ½ cup.

THE PACIFIC NORTHWEST SEAFOOD COOKBOOK

TOMATO SALAD

2 cups diced tomatoes

1 teaspoon fish sauce

1 teaspoon kosher salt

3 garlic cloves, minced

2 tablespoons rice vinegar

1 tablespoon chopped chives

In a small bowl, combine the tomatoes, fish sauce, salt, and garlic. Stir and let it sit for 2 minutes, then mix in the vinegar and chives.

SHRIMP:
OUR DANGEROUS
ADDICTION

Seafood eaters in the United States have a shrimp problem, and it's not just that we don't know the difference between shrimp and prawns (more on that later)—it's that we're addicted to bad shrimp. We import almost 1.5 billion pounds of shrimp each year, and most of that imported shrimp is unsustainably harvested, of poor quality, and produced by dubious labor practices. This is one of the reasons that you should feel good about eating seafood caught in the United States: our fisheries management system monitors for such abuses of workers and the environment. (If you have a chance, read the Pulitzer Prize–winning 2016 expose "Seafood from Slaves" on shrimp slave labor from the Associated Press.) In short: if you're eating imported shrimp, you're probably eating climate-destroying slave shrimp.

I have made very few strong stands in this book (as it covers only sustainable seafoods), but I beg of you, dear readers, if you make no other change in your seafood scarfing: eat wild American shrimp. Even leaving slave labor and cesspool production practices aside, the flavor of PNW shrimp simply can't be compared to the imported crap. It's closer to crab or lobster than it is to the junk coming in. Come, try it, and try not to be mad at the Pacific Northwest for hiding its stash of wild, sustainable, sweet-as-sugar shrimp and prawns.

There are a handful of varieties in the region, but the two major ones that you'll find on menus and in seafood shops are the big, rich spot prawns and the teeny-tiny, but equally sweet, pink shrimp. But first, as promised: what's the difference between shrimp and prawns? Scientifically, they're different suborders: shrimp are Pleocyemta, prawns are Dendrobrachiata. In practice, that means shrimp have plate-like gills, while prawns have branching gills, and shrimp have claws on two legs, with the largest pincers in front, while prawns have claws on three legs, and the second pincers are the largest—the list goes on. Exciting stuff, no? The reality is, when it comes to eating, they're the same thing. To make it extra fun, spot prawns are actually shrimp. Seriously, don't worry about this: whatever you call them, they're delicious.

Spot prawns are the largest and most important shrimp in the region, growing up to 9 inches long. That's a whole lot of sweet, snappy-fleshed shellfish. The big shrimp are found in stores in one of two ways: alive and swimming or dead (fresh or frozen). Ideally, buy them live from a tank—that leaves the most options for eating, including lightly cured (as in the Spot Prawns Two Ways on page 163). Buying them live means you are guaranteed to get the head, too, which holds much of the flavor.

In general, avoid purchasing head-on spot prawns that are not alive in a tank: when spot prawns die, they immediately decay around the head and the meat will be corrupted. Purchase head-on spot prawns only if they are still alive and will stay so until you cook. Make sure to cook them as soon as possible, as more than a few hours in the refrigerator and they may die and begin to fall apart.

If you can't face having to keep a small sea creature alive for a few hours—or having to kill it yourself—purchase some dead spot prawns, which you'll have to do anyway when it's not the season (spring and summer). Fresh, frozen, or previously frozen spot prawns keep relatively well, as long as they're properly cared for. Usually that will mean head-off, but you may occasionally find head-on, frozen-at-sea (FAS) spot prawns for sale. Mostly shipped to Japan in this form, these shrimp were frozen while still fresh and will be a quality product if you defrost them in your refrigerator in a drip pan or in a colander placed in a bowl. Don't let them sit in their own liquid!

If you do purchase live ones, you can toss them in the freezer for a few minutes before you cook them to make it easier and more humane to kill them. Make sure they stay in the freezer only long enough to slow their movements and numb them, but not long enough to freeze them, about 5 to 7 minutes. The easiest way to kill them (and prep them) is to hold the head between your thumb and first two fingers of one hand and the body in the same fashion with the other and simply twist in opposite directions as you pull them apart.

On the complete other end of the spectrum from the fully alive spot prawns are pink shrimp. You'll sometimes see these called Oregon, bay, or salad shrimp, or some combination of the four terms, and they're the polar opposite of spot prawns: they're little tiny guys and are pretty much sold in stores only already cooked. Because they're rarely found in their raw form, all of the recipes here assume you are purchasing them cooked: they'll be headless, shell off, and ready to go. I usually rinse them right before I use them, but otherwise they can go straight from the refrigerator to the plate—which also makes them a great option for keeping in the freezer to quick-defrost for last-minute meals.

SALT-BAKED SPOT PRAWNS

SERVES 2 AS A LIGHT SNACK

As one of the purest tastes of the Northwest, spot prawns taste best with very little done to them. This gentle method just barely cooks the prawns, leaving them as close to nature as possible—with just a tiny bit of salt to bring out the flavor of the sea. The dish is doable with frozen, head-off prawns, but works best with live, head-on spot prawns. Either way, leave the shell on until after you cook it; otherwise they will end up way too salty.

3 pounds kosher salt

½ pound spot prawns in their shells

Preheat your oven to the highest temperature (usually around 500 to 550°F). Spread one-third of the salt on the bottom of a baking dish, making sure there is an unbroken layer big enough for all of the shrimp to lie on. Place the other two-thirds in a second baking dish, one that won't be too difficult to pour from. Place both baking dishes in the oven for at least 45 minutes (though longer is even better). When you are ready to remove the salt, have the prawns out and ready to go.

Working as quickly as possible, pull out the baking dish with the one-third layer and place the shrimp on it, making sure they're in a single layer. Pour the second dish of hot salt on top, making sure all the shrimp are completely encased in the salt. Use a spoon or other utensil to move the salt if needed. Leave the prawns in the salt for 4 minutes, then remove, peel (see page 159 for instructions), and serve them immediately. If you used live prawns, invite diners to suck out the flavorful meat in the head portion when they finish eating the body.

HONEY-WALNUT SPOT PRAWNS

SERVES 4

Chinese-style honey-walnut prawns fly off the dim sum carts in Seattle's International District, beloved for their crunchy nuts and sweet sauce. But the shrimp beneath the blanket of white sauce rarely deliver much flavor. In this version, the dish trades mass-market shrimp for wild local spot prawns, sheds the thick coating, and dials up the tang, while keeping the sweet crunch that made it so beloved in the first place. While this often comes alone as an appetizer-type portion at dim sum, at home it works well over rice and/ or broccoli for a dinner.

1 cup walnuts

⅓ cup sugar

¼ cup mayonnaise

Juice of ½ lemon

½ tablespoon honey

½ tablespoon sweetened
   condensed milk

1 teaspoon soy sauce

¼ cup cornstarch

¼ teaspoon kosher salt

1 pound spot prawns, peeled,
   deveined, and heads removed
   (see page 159)

½ cup vegetable oil

1 teaspoon chopped chives

Toast the walnuts in a dry, medium pan over medium heat, shaking the pan or stirring frequently, until they're fragrant and a shade or two darker—about 5 minutes. Remove the walnuts and add ⅓ cup of water, bringing it to a boil. Add the sugar and stir until it's dissolved. Keep stirring until the mixture darkens a few shades, about 5 minutes. Add the nuts back in, stirring to coat them completely. Transfer the nuts to a piece of parchment paper, using a spoon to separate them so they don't stick together, and let them cool. Don't stress too much if they do stick together: just let them cool a few minutes and then separate by hand.

In a large bowl, stir together the mayonnaise, lemon juice, honey, sweetened condensed milk, and soy sauce. Set aside.

On a plate or in a zip-top bag, mix the cornstarch and salt. Toss the prawns in the cornstarch mixture, coating each one completely.

Heat the oil on high in a large pan (it should fit all the prawns in a single layer). When the oil is spitting hot, lay each prawn into the oil, cook for about 90 seconds, then flip and cook another 90 seconds. Transfer the cooked shrimp directly into the mayonnaise mixture, and toss. Add the walnuts and toss again. Sprinkle with the chives and serve immediately.

HOW TO PEEL AND DEVEIN SPOT PRAWNS

To prepare the spot prawns for this recipe, follow the instructions on page 154 to kill the prawns. Then lay the prawn on its back and use your thumbs to push the edges of each side of the shell and legs outward. You should be able to tear the shell off in this fashion—pulling the shell in a circular direction. The first few bits of shell should come off pretty easily, then you can pinch the tail and twist the meat out, much like how you twisted the head off. Finally, make a shallow incision running down the back and pull out the vein that runs the length of the shrimp.

SHRIMP BISQUE

SERVES 4 TO 6

Inspired by their cross-country rivals, Gulf shrimp, spot prawns take up residence in this New Orleans-style shrimp bisque. The simple soup takes its thickness from a scoop of rice instead of a roux, giving it an unexpected heartiness. Meanwhile, the flavor comes from roasting the shells of the same shrimp that get tossed in.

4 tablespoons (½ stick) unsalted butter

1 pound spot prawns, peeled and shells reserved, deveined, and heads removed (see page 159)

2 bay leaves

1 yellow onion, chopped

1 celery rib, sliced

1 carrot, sliced

1 teaspoon kosher salt, plus more as needed

¼ cup sherry

1 tablespoon tomato paste

3 sprigs thyme

3 sprigs parsley

¼ to ½ teaspoon cayenne pepper, depending on spice preference

¼ cup rice (preferably long grain)

Juice of ½ lemon

Freshly ground black pepper, as needed

½ tablespoon chopped chives

¼ cup crème fraîche (optional)

Melt 2 tablespoons of butter over medium-high heat in a large pot, then add the shrimp shells. Cook, stirring occasionally, until the shells have darkened to a deep red, almost brown, about 5 minutes. Add 5 cups of water and 1 bay leaf, bring it to a boil, then turn it down to a simmer for 30 minutes. Strain, reserving the stock and discarding the shells. Once you set aside the stock, you can reuse the same pot.

Over medium heat, add 1 tablespoon of butter and cook the shrimp just until they turn completely opaque, about 3 to 5 minutes. Remove and chop them roughly.

Keeping the medium heat, add the remaining tablespoon of butter. When melted, add the onion, celery, carrot, and 1 teaspoon of salt, and cook, stirring occasionally, until soft, about 10 minutes. Add the tomato paste and let it darken for another minute or 2.

Deglaze the pan with the sherry, pouring it in and using your spoon to pull up any of the flavorful bits stuck to the pan. Let it evaporate for 3 to 5 minutes.

Tie the thyme, remaining bay leaf, and parsley together (or put in a large tea ball or any other way that will make them easy to remove later). Add the shrimp shell stock, this bundle, the cayenne, and rice. Bring it to a boil, then turn to low heat and let it simmer until the rice is soft, about 20 minutes.

Stir in half of the chopped shrimp, remove the bundle of herbs, and blend (this is easiest with an immersion blender). Add the lemon and season with salt and pepper to taste.

Split the bisque into bowls and garnish each bowl with the remaining shrimp, chives, and, if using, a dollop of the crème fraîche.

SPOT PRAWNS TWO WAYS

SERVES 6 AS A LIGHT APPETIZER OR 2 AS A LIGHT MEAL WITH RICE

MUTSUKO SOMA | KAMONEGI | SEATTLE

While Mutsuko Soma's culinary reputation mostly revolves around the fresh soba noodles she rolls out each day in her restaurant, many of the gems on her menu involve her reverent, delicate treatment of seafood. For this recipe, she uses a technique called kimi zyoyu (or soy sauce and egg), to quick-cure the prawn bodies, then creates a warming miso soup from the heads to wash it down. And once you sip the soup, "you have to suck the heads," she says. "It's mandatory."

If you are serving this as a meal, lay the tails on a bed of rice. Either way, start with the prawn tails, then follow with the soup—and don't forget to suck those heads.

6 live spot prawns

1 egg yolk

1 teaspoon soy sauce

3 sprigs chives

2 tablespoons white miso paste

1 bunch scallions, thinly sliced

Cut off the heads of the prawns and set them aside for the soup. Peel the bodies, leaving the tails on (see page 159 for instructions).

Mix the egg yolk and soy sauce in a small bowl. Stir vigorously a few times until it emulsifies. Dredge each spot prawn through the dressing and refrigerate for at least an hour before serving, or as long as overnight. When serving, lay the prawns on a plate or rice bowl, drizzle on the remaining dressing, and top with chives.

Bring a cup of water to a boil in a small saucepan. While it heats, trim the whiskers from the prawn heads (easiest to do with scissors or kitchen shears). Then, when the water is at a boil, add the heads. Cook for 1 minute, then turn off the heat.

Add the miso to a large ladle that fits into the pot of water and lower it down. Once it's submerged, use a spoon or chopsticks to agitate the miso, letting it slowly melt into the water as you break up chunks. Once the miso is evenly incorporated, the soup is ready to serve. Top with a generous handful of scallions.

SHRIMP ROLLS

SERVES 4

Lobster rolls are the quintessential East Coast seafood dish, but here on the West Coast there's no such signature dish. Some people like to pop crab in, which works, but I find that tiny bay shrimp give the same supple sweetness that makes lobster so delightful when sauced in mayonnaise and wrapped in a bun—and, unlike lobster, bay shrimp cost very little. These go very well with potato chips, particularly the pride of the Northwest, Tim's Cascade.

1 pound cooked bay shrimp

6 tablespoons mayonnaise

4 scallions, thinly sliced

6 sprigs tarragon leaves, chopped

Zest and juice of ½ lemon

1 celery rib, thinly sliced

¼ teaspoon kosher salt

Freshly ground black pepper, as needed

4 brioche or Hawaiian sweet roll hot dog buns (see note)

4 to 8 leaves little gem or butter lettuce (depending on size)

Mix the shrimp, 4 tablespoons of mayonnaise, the scallions, tarragon, lemon zest and juice, celery, and salt. Grind a hefty amount of black pepper on top.

Spread the remaining 2 tablespoons of mayonnaise on the hot dog buns (if you don't have top-split buns, you likely won't need quite as much). Place the buns under the broiler for about 3 minutes, until caramel-brown and lightly crisp.

Line each bun with lettuce leaves, then fill with the shrimp mixture.

Look for top-split brioche buns or the King's Hawaiian sweet roll hot dog buns, which come top-split—meaning a little more outside surface for crisping up.

BAY SHRIMP LOUIE

SERVES 4 AS AN ENTRÉE, 8 AS AN APPETIZER

Depending on your source, the classic crab Louie salad was invented in either Seattle or San Francisco, but regional loyalty requires me to believe the former version. The story goes that it was invented at Seattle's Olympic Club in 1904, and famed opera singer Enrico Caruso so enjoyed it when he was in town that he ordered and ate the salad until there was none left. Regardless of the truth behind the legend, one of the biggest fans of the salad was Oregon's own James Beard.

For this version, though, I take the bay shrimp from Beard's home state and sub them in for the crab, making it more affordable, but equally (if not more) delicious. Presenting it as a wedge salad, as described below, works well when serving four, but for a larger crowd, cut up the lettuce and serve it as a chopped salad.

2 eggs

1 iceberg lettuce head

1 large avocado

2 cups cherry tomatoes, halved

1 pound cooked bay shrimp

Louie Dressing (recipe follows)

1 tablespoon chopped parsley

1 lemon, in wedges

Bring a pot of water to a boil over medium heat and gently lower in the eggs. Boil them for 10 minutes, then transfer them to a bowl of ice water. Peel and quarter.

Cut the lettuce into wedges. Cut the avocado in half, and then slice it.

Arrange the salad with the wedges on their side, topped with the avocado, tomatoes, egg, and shrimp.

Dollop on the dressing and sprinkle it with the parsley. Serve with the lemon wedges. Squeeze the wedges over the shrimp before eating.

LOUIE DRESSING

½ cup mayonnaise

2 tablespoons chile sauce

1 tablespoon Tabasco or similar
    hot sauce

1 teaspoon Worcestershire sauce

Juice of ½ lemon

Mix all the ingredients together.

CLAMS:
FROM FAMILIAR
TO WEIRD

When it comes to Pacific Northwest clams, Manilas dominate, though the giant geoduck—with a sizable reputation to match—gets most of the gawking attention.

How could it not? Everything about the geoduck incites giggles, from its name—pronounced goo-ee-duck—to its suggestive shape. The only thing about geoducks that is no-nonsense is trying to pull the foot-plus long clams from their deep burrows in tidal waters. Like elephant snouts, the clam is thick and muscular, a texture that can be off-putting for some. But in raw preparations, like geoduck sashimi, or when used carefully, it offers a chew-crunch combination with an overwhelmingly delightful taste of the sea. Sadly, aside from stuffed-animal versions like the local Evergreen State College's mascot, you don't see much geoduck in stores.

The razor clam, however, is much like a mini-geoduck, easier to find in stores, and far simpler to dig for yourself. The Washington Department of Fish and Wildlife's website has complete information on when, where, and how to dig for razor clams, which mostly requires a $30 clam "gun," a fishing license, and a willingness to drive out to the coast on the designated day. In return, you can collect as many as 15 of the clams, which range from the size of two fingers to an entire hand. The site also includes insight into the slightly time-consuming cleaning process. The resulting meat, though, is worth the trouble. The foot is tender and flavorful when fried up (page 183), and the body makes a killer Clam Risotto (page 182), chowder, or stir-fry.

Mostly, though, when we talk clams in the Northwest, we're talking about Manilas, "the unsung hero of Pacific Northwest shellfish," according to Shina Wysocki of Chelsea Oyster Farms. A stowaway accidentally imported from Japan on oyster seed, the small, oblong Manila clam found a welcoming home in the region, joining native species like the littleneck and butter clams. But the littleneck doesn't gather much attention because of its shorter shelf life and longer cooking time than the otherwise similar Manila, and the butter clam gets ignored because it tends to accumulate toxins.

Quick to grow (about two years to get to market size), fast to cook (a whole dinner in less than 10 minutes), and one of the simplest, most affordable types of seafood to find, Manilas are one of the easiest points of entry into Pacific Northwest shellfish. They're nutritious, have a long shelf life, and reproduce on their own, which makes them easy to farm.

If you're collecting them yourself, make sure you have a license to harvest and that you check for red tide warnings in the area where you are gathering.

Most places selling the clams should have already purged them (ask if you are unsure), but if you pluck them from the sand yourself, grab some of the same water they live in to use to purge them—just let them sit in the clean, sand-free water for at least four hours. "You'll see them spit out the sand," Wysocki says, so it's easy to know when they're ready. Assuming you're buying them, though, the main thing is to make sure they're closed tight, or that they shut themselves up when you touch. Then take a nice whiff: "They should smell like the sea, and nothing else," says Wysocki. "Avoid any funk."

Once you get them home, the best way to keep them is in a single layer (like on a sheet pan) with a damp cloth over top, in the coldest part of your refrigerator, then cook them when you're ready. But note, contrary to popular belief, a clam not opening in cooking doesn't mean something is wrong with it—it just needs to cook a little bit longer.

PACIFIC NORTHWEST STEAMED CLAMS

SERVES 10 TO 12 AS AN APPETIZER OR 6 AS AN ENTRÉE

BRENDAN MCGILL | HITCHCOCK RESTAURANT GROUP | BAINBRIDGE ISLAND, SEATTLE

Whenever my dad brought out the big wooden spider, its bowl made of intertwined wire, we knew it was clam night. Plentiful, affordable, and easy to make, steamed clams were a treat for our family of five. Nights ended with each of us hidden behind a midden-like stack of empty shells, dragging leftover bread through the briny butter left behind.

Brendan McGill—whose restaurant, Hitchcock, captures the flavor of Washington's seafood from its island perch—manages to take the flavor of my childhood memories and improve upon it, mostly via cultured butter, which is essential and a revelation in this recipe.

This recipe offers instructions on using a steamer pot insert, but any type of steamer will work, including the collapsible kind you can find in many grocery stores.

2 cups dry white wine (unoaked Chardonnay, ideally)

1 leek, white part only, thinly sliced

6 garlic cloves, halved, any hard stem removed, then sliced very thin

1 fresh bay leaf

1 lemon, quartered

1 tablespoon kosher salt

½ pound (2 sticks) cultured butter, room temperature, cubed and separated (see note)

6 pounds Manila clams, well rinsed and scrubbed

1 sourdough baguette

¼ bunch Italian flat-leaf parsley leaves, chopped (about ½ cup)

Put the wine, leek, garlic, bay leaf, lemon, salt, and 1½ sticks of cubed butter in the bottom of a steamer pot. Turn the heat to high for 3 to 5 minutes to burn the alcohol from the wine—a big whiff of the pot should not have any alcohol smell.

Add the steamer insert, with the clams inside, and cover. Every couple of minutes, lift the lid and check on the clams. Stir gently with tongs to redistribute the clams. Cook just until they open, which may be just a few minutes or as long as 10.

Make the bread while the clams are steaming. Cut the baguette lengthwise and spread on the remaining butter. Grill the bread on both sides over hot coals, or broil it in the oven, for about 5 minutes. Cut the bread into 2-inch chunks.

When the clams are done, remove the lid and garnish with the parsley. Serve the clams out of the pot or distribute in individual bowls with the broth and grilled bread for dunking.

Find cultured butter near the regular butter in most mid- or high-end grocery stores or gourmet or specialty shops.

RAINIER BEER, ROMANESCO, AND RAS EL HANOUT MANILA CLAMS

SERVES 4

ZOI ANTONITSAS | SEATTLE

Two Northwest specialties meet up in this dish: Manila clams and Rainier beer. The beer and Moroccan spice come together with the brown butter to give a lovely fall or winter feel to this nice dish to cozy up with—the torn bread really adds to the rusticity and makes you feel like you should be eating this in front of a roaring fire.

½ loaf crusty bread

4 tablespoons extra virgin olive oil

Kosher salt, as needed

1 head Romanesco florets, cut into bite-sized pieces (if unavailable, substitute cauliflower, broccoli, or a mix for about 4 cups)

4 tablespoons (½ stick) unsalted butter

3 garlic cloves, sliced

Set the oven to broil. Tear the bread into fist-sized pieces and place them on a sheet pan. Drizzle with 2 tablespoons of olive oil, sprinkle with salt, and toss them gently. Repeat that process with the Romanesco on a second sheet pan.

Place both sheet pans in the oven, with the Romanesco directly under the broiler. Broil for 5 minutes, then rotate the position of the two trays for another 3 to 5 minutes each, repeating until the bread and Romanesco are both just browned. Turn off the broiler, but leave the pans in the oven to stay warm as you cook the clams. (If you have a separate broiler, you want to broil the Romanesco for about 10 minutes, then put it in a low oven, about 300°F, while you broil the bread.)

2 pounds Manila clams, well
    rinsed and scrubbed
1 tablespoon ras el hanout (if you
    don't have it or can't find it, a
    good curry powder will do in
    a pinch)
6 ounces Rainier beer (or similar,
    such as Pabst Blue Ribbon)
Juice of 1 lemon
2 tablespoons chopped herbs
    (chives, parsley, dill, or
    similar)

In a large sauté pan or shallow pot, cook the butter on medium-high heat until it just starts to turn golden brown, about 3 minutes. Add the garlic and stir well.

Next, add the clams, ras el hanout, and a pinch of salt. Stir well, add the beer, and cover. Let it steam for about 5 minutes, until the clams have all opened. Remove the lid, add the Romanesco, squeeze in the lemon juice, and stir gently, letting it absorb for a minute or two. Serve immediately, garnished with fresh herbs and bread.

MANILA CLAMS WITH PEAS AND GREEN GARLIC

SERVES 4

JASON STRATTON | MBAR, MAMNOON | SEATTLE

As one of Seattle's smartest and most interesting chefs, Jason Stratton has helmed an Italian restaurant specializing in pasta, a Spanish restaurant, and a Middle Eastern spot, and has appeared on *Top Chef*. In this clam recipe, he takes a little from each of those cooking traditions and puts together a beautiful recipe showcasing his talent and the flavors of spring in the Pacific Northwest.

3 tablespoons extra virgin olive oil

3 to 4 stalks green garlic, white parts only, thinly sliced and rinsed under cold water

1 shallot, minced

1 bunch dill, chopped, with 1 tablespoon reserved

1 cup dry white wine

1 teaspoon Aleppo chile powder

1 pinch saffron

2 pounds Manila clams, well rinsed and scrubbed

1 cup shelled English peas, blanched and shocked

Heat the olive oil in a wide saucepan or Dutch oven over medium-low heat. Add the sliced green garlic and shallot and cook for about 6 minutes. Add all the dill (save 1 tablespoon) and keep cooking for another 6 to 9 minutes, until the garlic and shallot are softened but not browned, and the dill is emerald green.

Turn the heat up to medium-high and deglaze with white wine by pouring it into the pan and gently scraping up any bits stuck to the pan. Add the Aleppo chile powder and saffron and reduce the liquid by half.

Add the Manila clams and cover the pan with a tight-fitting lid. Cook for 3 to 4 minutes, until the clams have opened. Add the English peas, mint, the rest of the dill, and the butter and cook for another minute or 2 until the peas have warmed through. Taste the broth, and add salt as needed. Serve immediately in warmed bowls with crusty bread to dip in the broth.

2 tablespoons mint, roughly
    chopped
1 tablespoon unsalted butter
Kosher salt, as needed
4 slices crusty bread

BLACK BEAN CLAMS

SERVES 4

Perhaps I should have known that I was destined to write about food for a living when a few friends and I instituted "Dim Sum Mondays" in high school—we'd all skip a class, head to the nearby International District, and take a long, early lunch over stuffed buns, dumplings, and, on occasion, black bean clams. I'm embarrassed to admit how far into adulthood I was before I learned just how easy that last dish is to make—certainly far easier than learning to pleat my own dumplings.

Although at dim sum we would eat these on their own, they go well over steamed bok choi or other greens, or over Chinese-style noodles or rice.

2 tablespoons vegetable oil

2 garlic cloves, chopped

1 teaspoon minced ginger (about ⅓ inch)

1 tablespoon salted black beans (see note)

2 tablespoons Shaoxing wine

2 pounds Manila clams, well rinsed and scrubbed

2 tablespoons oyster sauce

1 teaspoon sugar

¼ teaspoon white pepper

1 tablespoon cornstarch

1 scallion, sliced

½ tablespoon chopped mint

1 small red chile, sliced thin (optional)

The black beans you need are small and hard, and will be from an Asian market or section of a store. They are not the canned or dried black beans you might find in Latin American stores. They will be labeled salted, preserved, or fermented. Any Chinese market should carry them and you can find them online.

Heat the oil over medium heat in a pan large enough to fit the clams in a single layer. Add the garlic and ginger, stirring as they cook until they're fragrant but not browning, about 3 to 4 minutes.

Mash the beans with a fork and add them to the pan with the wine, clams, and ½ cup of water. Cover and turn the heat to medium-high, cooking until all the clams open—about 5 to 7 minutes.

Use a slotted spoon to remove the clams to the serving plate (or to a bed of rice, noodles, or vegetables). Try to position the clams so they gape up as much as possible.

Add the oyster sauce, sugar, and white pepper to the pan and let it reduce for 2 minutes. Mix the cornstarch with 2 tablespoons of water, then add that slurry as well, stirring for just a second as it thickens. Spoon the sauce over the top of the clams, then sprinkle the scallion and mint as a garnish—and the red pepper if you'd like a little heat.

RAZOR CLAM RISOTTO

SERVES 4

Digging for razor clams is messy—and cleaning them is messier still. Yet the end result is worth it: the soft foot of the clam and the slim body bring the light flavor of the ocean right to the table with a crisp seafood snap. But they do best in separate dishes: while many razor clam recipes have you use both parts together, they have entirely distinct textures that deserve completely different treatment.

6 cups chicken stock

5 tablespoons unsalted butter

1 yellow onion, diced

1½ cups Arborio rice

½ cup white wine

15 razor clam bodies (without diggers) or about 10 whole clams (see note)

¼ cup grated Parmesan

½ teaspoon kosher salt, plus more as needed

Freshly ground black pepper, as needed

Heat the stock and leave it over low heat as you cook.

Melt 4 tablespoons of butter over medium-low heat, then add the onion and cook until it's just translucent, about 5 minutes. Add the rice and sauté for a minute before adding the white wine.

Add a ladleful (about ½ cup—no need to be exact) of the stock to the rice, stirring a few times and waiting until it is absorbed. Repeat with more ladles until the rice is fully cooked (about 40 minutes). You might not use quite all the stock, but better to have too much than too little. At the end, it won't be able to absorb any more liquid and the rice will be soft.

Stir in the clams and cheese, the remaining tablespoon of butter, and then salt and pepper to taste. By the time the stirred-in butter has melted, the clams will be cooked (it's just a few seconds, really), and you're ready to eat.

These recipes use 15 clams as the measurement, as that's the limit in Washington from one day of digging; but if you're buying from the store, 1 pound will be about 8 to 12 clams, and it should be fine for either this recipe or the following one—neither is exacting.

> **HOW TO CLEAN RAZOR CLAMS**
>
> To clean your clams, give them a quick dip (5 seconds) in boiling water, then move them to an ice bath. The shells should slip right off. Then you'll want to snip off just the tip, at the end of the siphon. The clam will move, and it seems a bit creepy. Now use scissors to cut down the body, the length of the clam, and remove the insides. Cut the plump foot or digger from the body. Give the foot a little squeeze and cut out the dark stomach. It may also shoot out the wormlike digestive enzyme (yup, just as gross looking as it sounds); toss that out, too. Cut the digger open and remove any remaining dark (sand) patches.

PANKO-CRUSTED RAZOR CLAM FEET

SERVES 4

The tender feet or diggers of razor clams (see page 182 for how to clean them) can be a little weird and mushy looking, but the contrast of the crunchy panko crust hides the visual reminder of what strange creatures they are, while giving them a fantastic textural combination. Unlike some of the other fried dishes in the book, you'll be able to shallow fry these, which makes everything a little neater and easier.

½ cup all-purpose flour

2 eggs, beaten

2 cups panko (Japanese) breadcrumbs

15 razor clam feet (see page 182 for instructions on cleaning and separating feet)

1 cup vegetable oil

Kosher salt, as needed

Tartar sauce, for serving

Place the flour, eggs, and panko each on its own plate. Move the feet through, first dusting them in the flour and shaking them off, then dipping them into egg, letting the excess drip away. Using your other hand, remove the clams from the egg and roll them through the panko, pressing on as much panko as you can get to stick onto them. Lay them on a sheet pan and refrigerate for 30 minutes.

Heat the oil to 375°F in a large pan. Set up a rack or paper towel to drain the clams on after frying. When the oil is hot enough, gently lower in half the clam feet and cook until they're golden brown, about 45 to 60 seconds depending on size. Flip and let them brown on the second side, another 30 to 45 seconds. Transfer to the rack or paper towel and sprinkle with salt. Repeat with the second batch of clams.

Serve with tartar sauce for dipping.

GEODUCK SASHIMI

SERVES 2 TO 10 AS A LIGHT APPETIZER

Geoduck, the great joke of the Pacific Northwest: a giant clam most often identified as "the one that looks like . . ." Yes, geoduck is an enormous phallic clam. It grows just below the sand and requires almost your whole body to dig up, and then once you have it in your hands it wriggles and mocks you, as a local might if you pronounce the name "jee-oh-duck" rather than "goo-ee-duck." They are, in a word, absurd.

And when you get them home to cook, the ridiculousness doesn't stop—peeling a geoduck, a necessary step in preparation, requires an action not unlike pulling off soggy pantyhose.

If you do manage to get your hands on a geoduck, though, don't let this task deter you—it's pretty simple and the resulting flavor is a pure expression of the Pacific Northwest.

1 geoduck (see note)

1 tablespoon soy sauce

½ tablespoon rice vinegar

½ teaspoon sugar

1 lemon, in wedges

When you bring home your live geoduck, DO NOT rinse it with fresh water until you are about to cook it. Even a splash of fresh water will kill a geoduck immediately, so if it is sandy, leave the sand in place until you are ready to prep and eat the giant clam. Likewise, do not store it on ice—a bowl in the refrigerator will do.

Bring a pot of water big enough to submerge the clam to a boil over high heat. Prepare an ice bath for after the boil.

While that comes to a boil, here's a quick note on geoduck anatomy: the long, skinny part sticking up out of the shell is called the siphon, ending in the tip. The wider section, mostly in the shell, is the body. But, as you'll discover, that's really almost a c-shape, surrounding the organs.

Use a small knife to gently trace along both sides of the shell to separate the body from it and shuck the entire clam out. The c-shape part that was previously in the shell will hold a mess of innards; remove them (they should pull right off) and discard.

Submerge the geoduck in the boiling water for about 30 seconds, then transfer it to the ice bath.

Once cool (a minute or 2 is fine), you should be able to loosen the skin on the body (the part that was in the shell) with your hands and then peel the skin off as if you're taking of a pair of tights, all in one piece.

The body is less commonly eaten, though it can be. For this dish, though, you'll want to use just the siphon: the long thin trunk that stuck up out of the shell. Cut off the body, so you just have that cylindrical part, and then cut off the very tip, too—it might be slightly darker.

recipe continues

CLAMS   185

Inside the siphon, you'll see two hollow channels. Cut the whole thing lengthwise through one side and the part separating the two channels, so that you could open it like a book and no longer have separated channels. This allows you to get in and make sure to rinse out any loose sand.

Before you cut the clam, set up a bed of ice—ideally crushed. Fold the geoduck siphon back over—closing the book, as if you hadn't cut it lengthwise, then use a very sharp knife to slice the geoduck siphon extremely thin—as thin as you can—setting the pieces on ice as they come off. The flavor is much more balanced and subtler the thinner you slice, so use a sharp knife and aim to get as close to paper-thin as you can.

Mix the soy sauce, rice vinegar, and sugar together. When ready, squeeze lemon juice over the clam, dip it lightly into the sauce, and eat.

OYSTERS:
START SMALL

"When the tide is out, the table is set," goes a traditional saying of the Coast Salish people. Oysters, many of which live on that tideline, bring the briny sweetness of saltwater to the plate, dragging with them, in their shells, the history of the region. The oldest middens, or mounds of discarded shells, in the Pacific Northwest indicate that Coast Salish people have been slurping the native Olympia species for more than 10,000 years.

Today, five different species of oyster grow in the Northwest, labeled with the names of dozens of inlets and companies, making it somewhat difficult to sort out what exactly you're buying or eating. Olympias, the West Coast's only native oyster, however, are almost always labeled as such. Tiny, barely bigger than a quarter, with a coppery, metallic flavor, they brought the reputation for great oysters to the region. They were shipped south to California during the Gold Rush and brought a rush of their own as the Olympia Oyster Company started in 1878, followed closely by other companies, including the Taylor family, whose Taylor Shellfish Farms is now on its fifth generation of oyster farming.

These days, Taylor sells all types of oysters: Virginica, a species originally from the East Coast, now grown here; a Japanese import called Kumamoto; and a wide variety of Pacific oysters. Brought to the region in 1919 by shellfish farmers looking for product easier to work with, the Pacific oysters account for likely more than 98 percent of Washington oyster sales. Whether called Hama Hama, Treasure Cove, Shigoku, or Chelsea Gem, these cucumber-bright oysters come in all sizes.

The Chelsea Gem comes from Chelsea Oyster Farms, where owner Shina Wysocki encourages Northwesterners to get out and meet their farmers. "Take a field trip!" she says. "Oysters speak of the land or water they're grown in." But even if you can't make it out to meet your oyster on the beach, she says the most important part of buying oysters is knowing where they come from. "The person you buy from should know the farm they came from and when they were harvested," she says. (In fact, it's illegal for shellfish to be sold without the vendor having a tag denoting just those things.)

When buying oysters in their shells, check that they are closed all the way, and that they aren't older than a week (and won't be by the time you eat them). Neither you nor the place you buy them should store them in water that isn't the saltwater they grew in—it can change the flavor. Keep them in the refrigerator, not on ice (that's too cold for them), and cover with a damp towel. If they open up, tap them, and if they close, that means they're still okay to eat. For any cooked oyster dishes or a quick treat when you don't need to impress with a tray of freshly shucked oysters, jarred oysters make a fine buy—they save you the time of shucking, probably cost less, and will keep for a little bit longer.

Look for clean shells, which Wysocki says means that the farmer took the time to care for them. You may notice that some of the shells are craggy and fluted, while others are smooth and rounded. The latter are tumbled, meaning they grew suspended from a structure, rather than in tide flats. The process forces the oysters to grow a deep cup and a tough shell, which makes them easier to shuck and makes just minor tweaks to flavor—a little milder, a little sweeter. For newcomers to oysters, tumbled Pacifics are an easy entry point.

Wysocki recommends starting both shucking and eating with oysters smaller than 3 inches. But once you've mastered that, she tells people to think about them like wine: the farming method, the location they grew in, the variety, and the season all contribute to the flavor you taste.

A note on seasonality: what about the myth of only eating oysters in months that have an "r"? That was likely written before modern refrigeration and scientific advances: Wysocki sells more oysters in summer than any other season, in part because of how oyster farmers can manipulate them to be sterile, avoiding the mushiness and cloudiness of spawning season. Thus, Pacific Northwest oysters are in season all year long, though the variety, flavor, and shelf life may vary. Understand what you're eating, when and where it was harvested, and then, in Wysocki's words, "Make it part of your oyster adventure."

HOW TO SHUCK AN OYSTER

The best way to buy oysters is live in their shells, and once you do that, the only way to get them out is to learn to shuck them yourself. It's a skill—something anyone can do—but one which will be hard at first and get easier the more you do it. The first half-dozen will seem impossible, and the second will make you think hard about the Jonathan Swift quote, "It was a bold man who first ate an oyster." But then you'll get used to it. You'll start to see shucking as a part of eating the oyster, not unlike peeling a banana.

You will need an oyster knife, and I highly recommend starting with a glove—an old canvas gardening glove is great, but anything that will protect your non-dominant hand works. A kitchen towel will do in a pinch.

Start with an "easier" oyster: something with a deep cup and rounded edge—a tumbled oyster like a Chelsea Gem, Shigoku, or Blue Pool. It will be more comfortable in your hand and easier to see what you're doing.

Hold the oyster with the flat side up in your non-dominant hand, the big round edge toward your fingers, and the narrower end towards your wrist. Locate the "hinge" (the narrowest point where the top and bottom of the oyster meet) and insert the tip of your oyster knife there.

It will take a little bit of force, but you should be able to wiggle it in until it's stuck in there—like a lollipop—without needing to muscle it. Muscling it is how things slip and people get cut. If you can't get it in, pull out the knife and try again, rather than forcing it.

Once it's in, twist the knife back and forth, like you're turning a doorknob—you should feel a little "pop." That means you've done the hard part! The oyster is open now; you just need to cut the muscles. Keeping the knife as close to parallel with the top, flat part of the oyster (but inside it), sweep the knife through the oyster, which will cut the oyster free from the top.

Discard the top, and, if you'd like, wipe your knife off. Now run the knife between the oyster and the bottom shell, as close to the bottom as you can, to cut the muscle that connects them.

Now you are finished—slurp your oyster straight or use it in any of the recipes in this chapter.

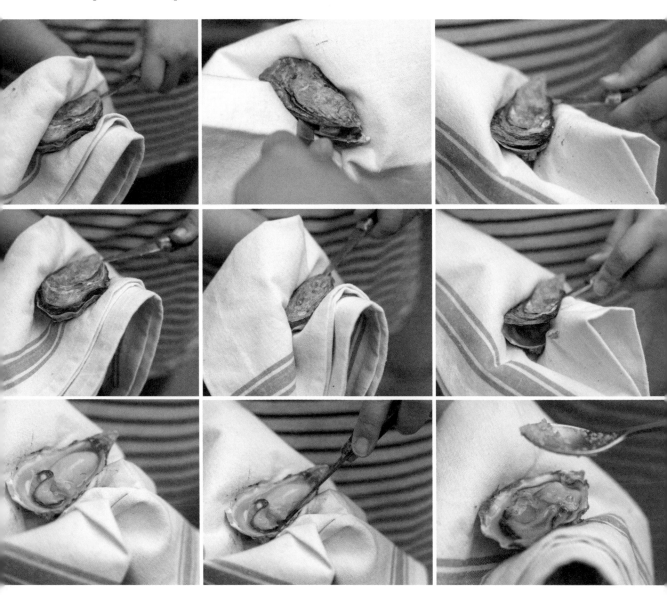

HANGTOWN FRY

SERVES 1

In the 1800s, the legend goes, a miner who had struck it rich wandered into Hangtown (now Placerville, California), and requested a restaurant to make him the most expensive dish the chef could manage. Bacon had to be delivered by ship around the tip of South America, eggs needed to be packed with incredible care as they traveled overland, and oysters had to be brought up from San Francisco on ice. So the chef created the Hangtown Fry.

By the middle of the 19th century, the dish made its way north to Seattle; but by the end of the 20th century, what was once an absurdly lavish and delightful dish had lost some of its luster and turned into a sorry diner-menu also-ran, made quick and gross.

This version takes inspiration from the original, using a little patience and extra effort to transform the no-longer-that-expensive ingredients into a breakfast that is rich only in flavor, and is perfect for the single diner!

2 slices thick-cut bacon

2 eggs, beaten

¼ cup breadcrumbs

3 small oysters, shucked

Cook the bacon in a medium pan over medium heat until nearly all the fat is rendered and the bacon is crisp. Remove the bacon from the pan.

Put the eggs in one bowl, pour the breadcrumbs into a second. Dip 1 oyster into the egg, letting the excess drip off, then roll it in the breadcrumbs. Repeat with the 2 remaining oysters.

With the bacon fat over medium-high heat, add the oysters, cooking them lightly, about 30 seconds each side.

Remove all but about 2 teaspoons of the bacon fat (it's okay, you can estimate it! Just leave a light layer on the bottom of the pans, so the eggs don't stick) and turn the heat to medium. Place the bacon in an "x" on one side of the pan and arrange the oysters around it. Add the eggs and cook without disturbing for about 2 minutes, until the eggs are just set.

Fold the egg from the egg-only side of the pan over the side with the bacon and oysters and cover the pan until the egg is fully cooked—another 2 minutes or so.

Transfer the eggs to a plate, ideally with the bacon side facing up.

GRILLED OYSTERS

SERVES 4 AS AN APPETIZER, 2 AS AN ENTRÉE

The first weekend in October is an exciting time: fall is sweeping in with magical colors, it's my birthday, and Shelton, Washington, hosts Oysterfest. For years I celebrated my birthday with a trek to the Olympic Peninsula to watch the fastest shuckers in the West, to slurp shooters, and to drink wine, often in the rain. My favorite stand, right at the entrance, was the Boy Scouts. They set up a giant grill for the oysters, covering them with wet burlap to keep them moist and slathering them in garlic butter before handing them over. Then, still standing feet from the grill, we'd suck them down before they even cooled off.

This is my best impression of those oysters. If you don't have a large swath of burlap, just use an old beach towel. Either way, I recommend sucking them down straight off the grill—this recipe works better for a casual gathering than a sit-down meal.

8 tablespoons (1 stick) unsalted butter, room temperature

6 garlic cloves, minced or pressed

24 medium live oysters, fresh and clean (see note)

Medium oysters are ideal, but if you're up for it, you can use bigger ones. I recommend saving the smaller ones for raw preparations (like the Dressed Oysters on page 199), as they'll dry out on the grill.

Preheat the grill to medium-high heat, about 425°F.

On the stove, heat the butter and garlic over medium-low heat, letting it cook for about 10 minutes. Set it aside for serving.

Arrange the oysters, cup side down/flatter side up on the grill. The grates should help them balance so they don't lean one way or the other. Cover them with wet burlap or a wet beach towel.

I recommend grilling the oysters in waves—6 to 8 at time so they don't get cold as you shuck them. The oysters will take about 4 minutes to cook, more if they're a bit larger. They'll signal their readiness by loosening their top—you may hear a pop. Remove them to a plate. If you crumple up a big piece of foil, then partially smooth it out, it makes a great surface for holding the oysters upright.

recipe continues

As you remove the oysters from the grill, use an oven mitt to hold the oysters in one hand, while you use a paring knife or oyster shucker inserted at the hinge of the oyster to pop the top up (see instructions on how to shuck an oyster on page 192, but know this is an easier version of that). Cut the muscle attaching the oyster to the top shell. Discard the top shell and use the knife to cut the muscle on the bottom, taking care to preserve as much of the juice—oyster liquor—in the shell as possible, and leave the oyster inside. Top with a teaspoon of the butter mixture, letting it mix into the oyster juices. Serve immediately.

DRESSED OYSTERS WITH ROASTED PEPPER GRANITA

SERVES 4 TO 8

HENRI NOL | CHELSEA FARMS OYSTER BAR | OLYMPIA

Chef Henri Nol worked at some of Portland's hottest restaurants before making his way north to Olympia's Chelsea Farms Oyster Bar, where he mingles that experience with his Los Angeles upbringing, Mexican heritage, and the fresh shellfish from the restaurant's sibling farm.

This dish shows how that all comes together in a lightly spiced, cool topping that pairs impeccably with the brininess of the oysters, while still allowing their taste of the sea to come through.

There's a bit of prep work involved, but the results are worth it. If you're hosting a party, you'll already have plenty of the Ancho Oil: all you'll need to do is double (or triple) the oysters and granita. It's almost no more work to prepare this for 24 than it is for eight (well, other than the shucking). Either way, you end up with a stunning, bracingly refreshing set of oysters.

You will need to make the Ancho Oil a day ahead, so make sure to start early.

1 garlic head

1 tablespoon olive oil

1 Anaheim chile

3 scallions, chopped

1½ tablespoons chopped shallot
   (about half of 1 small shallot)

Juice of 1 lime

⅓ cup chopped cilantro

⅛ teaspoon kosher salt

24 small live oysters

Ancho Oil (recipe follows), as
   needed

Preheat the oven to 400°F.

Place the garlic on a piece of foil and drizzle with the olive oil. Wrap tightly and place it in the oven for 30 minutes. You'll have a lovely head of nicely roasted garlic, and you're only going to need 6 cloves for the recipe, so go ahead and spread some on toast to snack on while you cook.

Roast the chile in the flame of a gas stove or on foil under a broiler at medium heat until well-charred and soft, about

recipe continues

10 minutes. Transfer it to a zip-top bag and let sit for about 10 minutes. Pull off and discard the char, the stem, and the seeds, and add the pepper to a blender, along with 6 cloves of the roasted garlic and the scallions, shallot, lime juice, cilantro, and salt. Start slowly, then speed up until it's thoroughly blended. If it has a little trouble getting moving, don't hesitate to add a bit of water.

Pour the sauce onto a sheet pan or other shallow tray (ideally metal, definitely with raised edges), spread it thin, and place it in the freezer. After 10 minutes, use a fork to break it up and stir, then return it to freezer. Repeat as needed until it's rough and slushy, like a granita. If it's spread thin and on a metal sheet pan, you probably only need to stir once—you'll be able to pull it at 20 minutes—but you may need more time if using deeper vessels or other materials.

If you forget about it and it freezes stiff, just set it out to melt and stir with a fork until it gets to the right texture.

Shuck the oysters and top each one with about a teaspoon of the granita and a few drops of the Ancho Oil (more if you like spice!).

ANCHO OIL

You'll have a ton of this leftover. Luckily it's delicious, and you can use it in salad dressing, on top of noodles or sweet potatoes, or pretty much anywhere you want to add a little heat.

1 dried ancho chile

1 cup olive oil

Remove the seeds and stem from dried chile and grind to a mostly fine, somewhat flaky dust with a mortar and pestle or in a spice grinder. Put the oil and chile dust in a jar and shake to combine. Leave for 24 hours before using.

THE PACIFIC NORTHWEST SEAFOOD COOKBOOK

OYSTER FRITTERS WITH FENNEL SALAD

SERVES 4

LEXI | OLD BALLARD LIQUOR COMPANY | SEATTLE

When Scandinavian immigrants arrived in the Pacific Northwest, explains Lexi, they found wild foods similar to what they'd left behind. They were able to work local foods—like oysters—into their familiar Scandinavian cooking styles. This recipe came from her grandmother and goes back to at least the 1920s. "Occasionally, older guests will see this dish at my café and wax nostalgic." She considers it a prime example of what regional Northwest cuisine means to her.

You can serve the fritters with a dollop of mayonnaise, but, says Lexi, "No garlic aioli, no dried garlic, nada: Nordic-style cooking doesn't use garlic at all."

1¼ cups canola oil

Juice of 2 lemons plus zest of 1 lemon and 4 wedges

2 teaspoons creamed horseradish

1 teaspoon kosher salt, plus a pinch

½ teaspoon white pepper

2 fennel bulbs (reserve fronds as garnish)

4 extra-large oysters, shucked

2 eggs

1 cup crushed saltines (about 24)

Add ¾ cup of the oil, the lemon juice, horseradish, 1 teaspoon of salt, and the white pepper to a bowl and whisk vigorously into a vinaigrette.

Slice the fennel thin (ideally using a mandoline) and toss with the dressing.

Roughly chop the oysters. Whisk the eggs and the lemon zest together, then lightly toss them with the oysters. Add the saltines and let it stand for 5 minutes.

Heat the remaining ½ cup of oil in a large sauté pan. Pat the oyster mixture into four round, flat patties, about ½ inch thick. Pan fry until they are golden brown on both sides, about 6 to 7 minutes total.

Serve the fennel salad, topped with the fritter and garnished with the fennel fronds, with a wedge of lemon on the side.

CHANTERELLE MUSHROOM AND OYSTER STEW

SERVES 4 TO 6

Fall in the Pacific Northwest brings the smell of the forest into the city with the rain, and brings the city dwellers out to the forest in search of golden treasures: chanterelle mushrooms. This seasonal stew combines them with local oysters and a little cream for just the kind of cozy fall dinner the gray season demands.

This goes best with plenty of oyster crackers and a few dashes of Tabasco sauce.

4 tablespoons (½ stick) unsalted butter

½ pound chanterelle mushrooms, roughly chopped (about 3 cups)

½ teaspoon rosemary

¾ teaspoon kosher salt, plus more as needed

1 yellow onion, chopped

5 garlic cloves, chopped

3 celery ribs, diced

2 tablespoons all-purpose flour

1 cup dry sherry

One 8-ounce jar oysters or about 8 small oysters, with their liquor

Heat 1 tablespoon of the butter in a wide pan over medium-high heat, and add the mushrooms, rosemary, and ¼ teaspoon of the salt. Let them cook, stirring occasionally, until the mushrooms release all their water (about 2 to 3 minutes), then continue until they begin to brown and stick to the pan (about 5 minutes). Remove from the heat.

In a large pot, heat the remaining 3 tablespoons of butter over medium and add the onion, garlic, celery, and ½ teaspoon of salt, cooking until the vegetables begin to soften, about 5 minutes. Add the mushroom mixture and cook 5 more minutes, then sprinkle in the flour, stirring to prevent clumping. When the flour is evenly dispersed but not yet cooking, add the sherry. Stir as it cooks for about 5 to 8 minutes, until the alcohol smell has burned off.

1 cup heavy cream

1 cup milk

Freshly ground black pepper, as
needed

¼ cup chopped parsley

1 lemon, in wedges

Turn the heat to low and add the liquor (liquid) from the oysters, the cream, and the milk. Cover and let it simmer for about 30 minutes.

Add the oysters and let them cook until the edges get frilly, about 2 to 3 minutes. Grind in a generous amount of black pepper and add salt to taste. Garnish with parsley and a wedge of lemon.

MUSSELS:
CHEAP AND DELICIOUS

Farmed mussels are a fairly recent arrival on the Pacific Northwest food scene. Penn Cove Shellfish on Whidbey Island is the oldest commercial mussel farm in North America—and it's only been open since 1975, nearly 100 years after the first commercial oyster farms. They produce both of the species of edible mussels farmed in the Pacific Northwest: Baltic, which they brand as Penn Cove, and Mediterranean, which are found and farmed widely in the region. Both are available pretty much year-round and are equally easy to work with, affordable, sustainable, and delicious, which makes them an incredibly good option if you're new to cooking shellfish.

How Mediterranean mussels arrived in the Northwest is something like a slapstick comedy: accidentally transported from Europe to California on a boat, then mislabeled and shipped to the Northwest, where it turned out they were not Pacific blue mussels, but the Mediterranean species considered a delicacy across the Atlantic. In the chilly waters of Totten Inlet and around Puget Sound, they thrived, growing up plump and sweet.

For the foragers out there, collecting wild mussels (a third species) is as easy as picking the right beach and plucking them from the rocks. Make sure you have a license to harvest and that you check for red tide warnings in the area where you are gathering mussels. But all three types share general cooking and care recommendations—and a similar short shelf life.

Live mussels are a bit more fragile than clams or oysters, with thin, brittle shells and a propensity for going bad quite quickly. Plan to eat your mussels as soon as possible—more like live crab than like clams or oysters. If you do need to keep them at all, lay them on a sheet pan in the refrigerator with a damp cloth on top. Don't save them more than a day or two.

Mussels, unlike their fellow mollusks, require an extra step of preparation: debearding. It is an annoying, somewhat finicky task, but it is fairly simple and extremely necessary. Start by scrubbing the outside of your mussels, checking each one to make sure that it's either tightly closed or closes tight when touched. Most of the PNW mussels are farmed, meaning they grew hanging from a rope, and thus aren't too dirty.

Then check out the instructions below to learn to debeard and you're ready to cook. Mussels prefer gentle cooking styles, such as steaming or smoking, but they happily take on all sorts of flavors, so it's easy to experiment with anything from the Thai-style Red Curry Mussels on page 214 to the Northwest apple cider idea from chef John Sundstrom on page 216.

HOW TO DEBEARD A MUSSEL

Debearding a mussel—removing the steel wool–like tangle of what's called "byssus threads"—is one of those tasks where it seems like everyone just copied and pasted from what the last guy said about it. Take hold of the threads or beard in one hand, the mussel in the other, and pull. Great! You're done!

I think these people are all delusional. In my experience, this works well for about one in every five mussels. Which is not a great ratio. Or it results in my getting part of the beard, but not all, leaving a tiny thread that I can now not get off for the life of me, even with tools.

Sometimes, if you read deeper, you'll see recommendations of pliers. This is more my speed—the threads are stronger than most things you'd use pliers on. But there's a better tool that, if you've been listening, you likely already have in your fish-cooking arsenal: tweezers.

Hold the mussel in your non-dominant hand, with the hinge toward you and the beard toward the tweezers in your other hand. Firmly grasp the threads with the tweezers as close to the mussel as you can get, then, holding the tweezers perpendicular to the mussel, twist or roll them, still clasping the thread, toward you. It will gently pull the threads out every time.

If you've got any barnacles on them and want to remove those, too, just use the dull backside of a butter knife to nudge them off, then rinse—though that's cosmetic only, as they won't hurt you or change the taste of the dish.

MOULES MARINIÈRES

SERVES 4

The only thing fancy about this French classic is how it looks when finished—the black mussel shells speckled with green parsley and afloat in the creamy sauce. In reality, this dish requires just a few easy-to-find ingredients, barely more than 15 minutes to make—including all the chopping—and looks and smells amazing. If you're going for a stunner, you can remove the mussels prior to stirring in the cream, which will allow you to really whisk it together, but it's not necessary. And, of course, any recipe demanding only ½ cup of wine is also asking for that same wine to be served with the meal.

2 tablespoons unsalted butter

4 garlic cloves, sliced

1 shallot, sliced

½ cup dry white wine

2 bay leaves

1 sprig thyme

2 pounds mussels, debearded and scrubbed (see page 208)

Juice of ½ lemon

3 tablespoons heavy cream

Kosher salt, as needed

Fresh ground pepper, as needed

2 tablespoons chopped parsley

Crusty bread, for serving

Heat the butter over medium-high heat in a heavy-bottom pan. Sautée the garlic and shallot until fragrant and soft, about 5 minutes. Add the wine, bay leaves, and thyme, and reduce until the alcohol has burned off, about 3 to 5 minutes.

Add the mussels and cover until they open, about 3 to 5 minutes. Gently stir in the lemon juice and then the cream and heat until just warm, 1 or 2 minutes. Remove from the heat, salt and pepper generously to taste, and sprinkle with the parsley.

Serve with slices of crusty bread for dipping.

TEA-SMOKED MUSSELS WITH MAYONNAISE

SERVES 6 TO 8 AS A LIGHT APPETIZER

Smoke and seafood go together like fish and the sea, whether traditional lox for bagels or oysters cooked on the grill. This simple stovetop set-up lets you reap all the flavor benefits of smoking, but with none of the extra equipment or need to tend to a fire. And, on that lazy note: if making the mayonnaise sauce seems like too much work, the dish works nearly as well with the smoked oil stirred into the store-bought stuff. Either way, this makes for lovely predinner hors d'oeuvres or as a party snack.

If you're careful, you can break off only the top of the mussel shell and serve them in the bottom shell, with the mayo and saltines on the side. Alternatively, you can remove the mussel entirely and serve each one on an individual cracker with a drizzle of the sauce.

1 cup uncooked rice

1 cup loose black tea

2 tablespoons brown sugar

4 tablespoons sesame oil

1 pound mussels, debearded and
scrubbed (see page 208)

16 to 20 saltines, for serving

Mayonnaise (recipe follows), for
serving

Line a wok with foil—you'll need more later if your wok or steamer insert doesn't already have a cover. Add the rice, tea, and brown sugar and toss lightly. Cover with the top to a bamboo steamer, the wok lid, or, if need be, a tight layer of foil, and place it over medium-high heat for about 5 minutes.

Remove the cover from the wok, which should be smoking by now, and place the steamer inside. Put the sesame oil in a small heat-safe bowl and put it into the steamer. Arrange the mussels around it in a single layer and replace the cover. Cooking time will depend on your set-up and stove, but likely will take 15 to

recipe continues

20 minutes. Check on it every few minutes after 12. Mussels should open up and may darken a bit to orange.

When all mussels are open and plump, remove from the heat. If you won't be eating them right away, try to conserve the liquid from the shell and keep the mussels stored in it. And that sesame oil? Use it to make the mayonnaise, below, and serve with the mussels.

MAYONNAISE

1 egg yolk

Juice of ¼ lemon

Pinch of kosher salt, plus more as needed

4 tablespoons smoked sesame oil (from smoked mussels recipe)

Whip together the egg yolk, lemon juice, and salt. You may be able to do this in an immersion blender if you tilt the cup to get such a small volume blending. Drizzle the smoked sesame oil in slowly, a bit at a time, whipping furiously as you do. Mix until it's entirely incorporated, salt to taste, then use as a dipping sauce or to dress the mussels.

RED CURRY MUSSELS

SERVES 4

The Thai curry pastes that can be found at many grocery stores are miracle workers on seafood. When I was a kid, my mom would use them to dress up shrimp and serve over rice. This version uses mussels, but really, this recipe is more forgiving than maternity leggings. Use what you can, use what you have. If you can't find an ingredient, leave it out, use something else, don't stress. This is an anti-stress recipe.

You'll want to serve this with some sort of starch to soak up the delicious sauce—over rice works well, but a crusty baguette also does wonders.

One 13.5-ounce can unsweetened coconut milk

1 lemongrass stalk, white part only (about the bottom 4 inches), thinly sliced

2 shallots, sliced

3 garlic cloves, sliced

2 to 4 tablespoons red curry paste (see notes)

1 tablespoon fish sauce

3 lime leaves (see notes)

2 pounds mussels, debearded and scrubbed (see page 208)

¼ cup chopped cilantro

¼ cup chopped Thai basil leaves

1 lime, cut in wedges

Heat ¼ cup of the coconut milk over medium heat in a wide pan. When it begins to shimmer with heat, add the lemongrass, shallots, and garlic and cook, stirring occasionally, for 3 to 4 minutes. Add the curry paste and a second ¼ cup of coconut milk, stirring again to incorporate, for another 3 to 4 minutes.

Deglaze by adding the fish sauce and scraping up any stuck-on bits, then add the remaining coconut milk and lime leaves, stirring it all together.

When it begins to boil, add the mussels and stir gently but completely. Cover and leave for 5 to 8 minutes, depending on the size of your mussels, until all mussels have opened.

Remove from the heat, stir again, then garnish with cilantro, Thai basil, and lime wedges.

How much curry paste you need will, of course, depends on the brand. Start with a little, add more if desired. Four tablespoons, at least, of my favorite brand, Mae Ploy, will get you a very spicy broth—use caution. I've found that the plastic tubs (like Mae Ploy) work best. Thai Kitchen, in glass jars, and similar brands tend to be a little blander, but you can always adjust by adding more of the paste or supporting ingredients.

Lime leaves, for many years, were labeled by a name with a pejorative meaning. In recent years, the food industry has woken up a little bit, but hasn't settled on a standard. Thus the leaves you find may be labeled as Makrut, wild, Thai, or any number of other words. As long as it says lime leaf, that's what you're looking for.

MUSSELS WITH APPLE AND BACON

SERVES 2

JOHN SUNDSTROM | LARK | SEATTLE

At Lark, Sundstrom's much acclaimed Seattle restaurant, he translates moments in the Seattle year into dishes on the table. This quick dish speaks to fall in the Pacific Northwest, with crispy bacon bits, three different sources of apple flavor, and a touch of thyme. Serve it right from a pot in the center of the table while you watch the rain pour down in November—that's as Northwest as it gets.

4 ounces smoked bacon, cut into ¼-inch lardons

1 small shallot, sliced into thin rings

½ Granny Smith apple, peeled and cut into ¼-inch cubes

1 pound mussels, debearded and scrubbed (see page 208)

2 tablespoons dry white wine

2 tablespoons apple cider

1 tablespoon apple cider vinegar

¼ cup heavy cream

1 thyme sprig, leaves only

¼ teaspoon kosher salt

Freshly ground black pepper, as needed

4 thick slices country bread, toasted

Cook the bacon in a heavy-bottomed pot or Dutch oven over medium heat until it is rendered and crisp, about 12 to 15 minutes.

Drain off all but 1 tablespoon of the fat. If there's no fat left, add 1 tablespoon olive oil. Add the shallot and diced apple and cook until slightly caramelized, about 5 to 7 minutes.

Turn the heat to medium-high. Add the mussels and gently stir to coat them with the bacon, shallot, and apple.

Deglaze the pan by adding the white wine, apple cider, and apple cider vinegar and stirring up the bits stuck to the bottom of the pan. Let the liquid reduce slightly.

Add the cream, thyme, salt, and as much freshly ground pepper as you'd like. Cover and cook for 2 minutes, or longer if needed, until all of the mussels are open and the sauce is reduced and slightly thickened.

Remove from the heat and serve immediately with toasted country bread.

...AND

MORE

MULTI-FISH RECIPES AND OTHER SEA CREATURES

There is a literal ocean-full of edible sea creature out there, swimming, sitting, and growing off the coast of the Pacific Northwest, teeming through its rushing rivers, and carousing in its freshwater lakes. To cover the entire seafood panoply of the region would be to fill many volumes, often with forgotten, underutilized, or rarely used species. So, while this book mainly focuses on recipes featuring the big boys of the region's fisheries—salmon, halibut, crab, and other shellfish—I would be remiss to leave out the little guys or recipes that use multiple types of seafood. For instance, the smelt and sardines that are, again, quite literally the little guys, or the octopus who is not, but rarely shows up on Northwestern dinner tables. Or the sea urchin that food-lovers seek out as uni on restaurant menus, but so seldom bring into their homes. And of course the pink scallop, the only Northwestern scallop legal to harvest, and one which disappeared for two decades and was only recently revived. Not to mention a classic like Cioppino (page 222), and a dish that should be a classic, the Pacific Northwest Moqueca (page 224).

While it isn't possible to pay homage to every single creature in the sea, this chapter is a chance to include some of the Pacific Northwest's lesser-known kinds of seafood: foods that you'll rarely see in the supermarket (at least, as in the case of squid, not locally caught). Hopefully you'll use this as an opportunity, once you're more than comfortable with the marquee species, to expand your seafood cookery and fall in love with the forgotten fish. If not, you'll at least have an amazing pasta sauce (page 232) while you try.

CIOPPINO

SERVES 6 TO 8

While this wonderful seafood stew is definitively from San Francisco, it's too perfect for the Pacific Northwest's seafood to leave out. This stew came from the city's Italian fishermen, who used whatever little bits were leftover from the day's catch, along with canned tomatoes, a few herbs, and plenty of wine. Those origins should give a hint as to the flexibility of this recipe: use whatever seafood you have around, and don't feel beholden to the ratios or amounts listed here.

It's nearly essential to serve this with crusty bread that you can drag through the buttery broth.

8 tablespoons (1 stick) unsalted
  butter

1 yellow onion, chopped

2 garlic cloves, sliced

1 celery rib, chopped

1 leek, white part only, chopped

1 fennel bulb, chopped

1 teaspoon kosher salt, plus more
  as needed

2 tablespoons tomato paste

1 tablespoon fennel seeds

One 28-ounce can crushed
  tomatoes

2 bay leaves

1 teaspoon oregano

1 teaspoon thyme

½ teaspoon cayenne pepper

1 cup dry white wine

½ pound clams, rinsed and
  scrubbed

½ pound mussels, debearded and
  scrubbed

½ pound spot prawns, peeled and
  deveined (see page 159)

½ pound fish (see note)

1 crab, cooked but still in the
  shell, separated into lumps

½ bunch parsley, chopped

Heat the butter over medium heat until melted. Add the onion, garlic, celery, leek, fennel, and salt. Stir until the vegetables begin to soften, about 5 minutes. Add the tomato paste and fennel seeds, and again stir for about 5 minutes, letting the tomato paste deepen in color a bit.

Add the tomatoes, 1 cup of water, and the bay leaves, oregano, thyme, cayenne, and wine. Once this comes to a boil, cover and let it simmer for about an hour.

Turn the heat back up to medium, stir in the clams and mussels and cover for 5 minutes. Then add the spot prawns, fish, and crab, and cover for 5 more minutes. Taste and adjust with salt and pepper as needed.

Garnish with the parsley.

Halibut works well here, but any white fish such as rockfish, cod, or lingcod works too, either from scraps (often very cheap at a fish market) or in about 2-inch pieces.

PACIFIC NORTHWEST MOQUECA

SERVES 6

EMME RIBEIRO COLLINS | ALCOVE DINING ROOM | SEATTLE

For many years, Emme Ribeiro Collins's parents ran the only homestyle Brazilian restaurant in Seattle—the only other options were steakhouses. When that closed, the trained chef and one-time *MasterChef* competitor opened her own restaurant in the same space, featuring Afro-Brazilian food with a Pacific Northwest twist—like this version of moqueca. The fish stew, from Salvador in Brazil's Bahia state, gets a local spin, with halibut, clams, mussels, and a little fennel. The Dungeness crab plays wonderfully with the creaminess, and the whole medley—with the Brazilian-Style Rice below—makes a stunning centerpiece for a dinner party.

1 pound halibut, skin and bones removed, cut into 1-inch strips

½ pound spot prawns, peeled and deveined (see page 159)

3 garlic cloves, minced

1 tablespoon extra virgin olive oil

Kosher salt, as needed

¼ cup palm oil (see note)

1 large yellow onion, sliced

½ fennel bulb, trimmed, cored, and sliced

One 13.5-ounce can unsweetened coconut milk

2 tablespoons lime juice

½ pound Manila clams, rinsed and scrubbed

Season the halibut and prawns with the garlic, olive oil, and salt lightly, and set aside.

Heat the palm oil in a large heavy-bottomed pot over medium heat. Add the onion and fennel and sauté until they begin to soften. Season generously with salt. Add the coconut milk and lime juice and simmer until the sauce is well incorporated.

Add all of the seafood, green peppers, tomatoes, half of the cilantro, and ¼ cup water and season with salt.

Bring the mixture to a simmer over medium heat. Reduce the heat to low and cook without stirring until the seafood is cooked through and the flavors blend, about 20 minutes. Add the remaining cilantro just before serving over the rice.

This recipe calls for palm oil (available at many supermarkets and online) and using it truly makes a difference. However, use the same caution you do in searching for sustainable seafood in checking that you find a sustainable palm oil.

½ pound mussels, debearded and
scrubbed

½ pound Dungeness crabmeat
(from about 1 crab)

1 green bell pepper, seeded and
de-stemmed, sliced

3 Roma tomatoes, sliced

¼ cup cilantro, chopped

Brazilian-Style Rice (recipe
follows), for serving

BRAZILIAN-STYLE RICE

¼ cup vegetable oil

3 garlic cloves, minced

2 cups jasmine rice

Kosher salt, as needed

Heat the oil over medium-high heat. Add the garlic and sauté, stirring until it begins to caramelize, about 30 seconds. Add the rice and salt. Sauté the rice for about 2 minutes, continuously stirring. At this point you can place the sautéed rice and 3 cups of water in a rice cooker or pour 3 cups of water into the pan and cook over medium heat until the rice is cooked through, about 15 minutes.

PINK SCALLOP CEVICHE AND LECHE DE PALOMA COCKTAIL

SERVES 8 TO 10 AS A LIGHT APPETIZER

Pink scallops, once a prized delicacy of the Pacific Northwest, are on their comeback tour: fishing for them has recently been revitalized and the tender, subtle shellfish returned to stores and tables. But few recipes exist after their two-decade disappearance. In this one, they nestle into the trappings of ceviche, inspired by the flavors used in Peru, and the garnish—popcorn—served with the dish in Ecuador.

Leche de tigre is the Peruvian name for the liquid leftover from ceviche, often considered a hangover cure. Here, it's woven with the flavors of a paloma, the classic cocktail of tequila and grapefruit soda, for a spicy, smoky, refreshing drink that matches the beautiful pink color of the scallop shells.

2 to 3 garlic cloves, minced

1 shallot, thinly sliced

1 tablespoon chopped parsley

Juice of 4 limes

Juice of ½ pink grapefruit

1 serrano pepper, de-seeded and
    very thinly sliced (optional)

1 pound pink scallops

1 tablespoon canola oil

2 tablespoons popcorn

Kosher salt, as needed

In a large bowl, stir together the garlic, shallot, parsley, lime juice, grapefruit juice, and—depending on your spice tolerance—pepper. The entire pepper will give you a big spice, a few slices a pleasant burn, but it can be omitted entirely for less spice-tolerant eaters (pepper slices can also be served on the side).

Shuck the scallops in their entirety from the shell—roe and muscles and all—and chop lightly, then add to the juice mixture. Let it sit for at least 20 minutes.

recipe continues

While the ceviche marinates, heat the oil in a small pot, with a single popcorn kernel. When it pops, add the rest of the kernels. When all kernels have popped (2 to 3 minutes), remove them from the heat and sprinkle with salt.

Wash the shells from the scallops and spread them on a plate, turning a few upside down to show off the color. When the ceviche is ready, spoon a dollop of it into each shell for serving, reserving the liquid—leche de tigre—for the cocktail that follows.

LECHE DE PALOMA

This recipe makes two cocktails, which is how much you will be able to shake at a time. You may have enough leche de tigre to make a few more cocktails, so it's just a matter of squeezing more grapefruit and shaking more drinks!

Juice of 1 pink grapefruit

½ cup leche de tigre

½ cup mezcal (look for a smoky reposado, if you have options)

2 parsley stalks, for garnish

Shake the juice, leche de tigre, and mezcal with ice. Strain and serve in a rocks glass over fresh ice, with a stalk of parsley to garnish.

INDONESIAN GRILLED SCALLOP POUCHES

SERVES 4

PAT TANUMIHARDJA

Born in Jakarta to Indonesian-Chinese parents and raised in Singapore, Pat Tanumihardja now lives in DC. But in between all those, Tanumihardja lived in the Pacific Northwest—where her parents ran a short-lived but acclaimed Indonesian restaurant. Now she's a food writer and cookbook author: *Farm to Table Asian Secrets: Vegan and Vegetarian Full-Flavored Recipes for Every Season* and *The Asian Grandmothers Cookbook*. She offered up this recipe, from her own mother, to show off the intersection of Pacific Northwest and Indonesian food.

Banana leaves, Tanumihardja explains, imbue a delightful fragrance to seafood on the grill. Firm fish, shrimp, mussels, and clams all benefit from this traditional method of grilling, so you can switch out for whatever you've got. If you can't find lemon basil, then Thai or Italian basil is just fine.

2 pounds pink scallops, shucked

Juice of 1 lime

1 small yellow onion, chopped (about 1 cup)

1 red or yellow bell pepper, chopped (about 1 cup)

2 large garlic cloves, sliced

1 cup lemon basil

2 teaspoons ground coriander

2 teaspoons sambal oelek (see note)

½ teaspoon kosher salt

4 banana leaves (10 by 15 inches; see note)

¼ cup chopped cilantro

Toss the scallops with the lime juice.

Heat the grill to medium (about 400°F).

Pulse half of the onion, half of the bell pepper, and the garlic in a food processor until finely chopped.

Mix the scallops with the processed onion mixture and the remaining onion and bell pepper in a large mixing bowl.

Add the basil leaves, coriander, sambal oelek, and salt, and toss until completely combined.

Place one banana leaf on a 12-by-16-inch piece of foil. Spread half of the scallop mixture in the center of one leaf. Cover it with a second banana leaf and another 12-by-16-inch piece of foil.

Roll the edges of the two pieces of foil together tightly to form a pouch. Repeat with the remaining banana leaves, seafood, and foil.

Grill the pouches with the grill lid on for about 8 to 10 minutes. Rotate the pouch halfway through to cook more evenly.

Remove the pouches from the grill. When they are cool enough to handle, take off the foil and place the pouches on serving plates. Slice each pouch open in the middle and peel back the leaf to expose the contents. Sprinkle with the cilantro and serve.

SEA URCHIN PASTA SAUCE

SERVES 2

Sea urchin, often called by its Japanese name, uni, because it's best known for its role at the sushi counter, is, like so much shellfish, better the closer you eat it to the sea. So, while you will see stacked trays of imported Japanese sea urchin, the true delicacy is the little green urchins and their larger red brethren plucked from Puget Sound and its environs. Inside the spikey exterior, the golden-orange pieces of uni sit just a few quick scissor snips away—ignore the fact that the part of the urchin we eat is the gonads as you dig into the relatively affordable luxury.

As with oysters, urchin lovers prefer them fresh and unadorned, just plucked from the shell. If that's you, ignore the ingredients after the urchin and stop after the first paragraph of instructions. But even I, an urchin purist, love blending it up with butter and stretching it out over a whole bowl of pasta. Okay, to be honest, I'll just buy twice as much uni and eat it both ways.

Some fish markets will do the job of cleaning the uni for you for a small fee, which can be worthwhile for the squeamish or those who don't like the idea of spikes all over their kitchen counter.

Kosher salt, as needed

1 pound in-shell sea urchin or 3 ounces shucked

3 tablespoons unsalted butter at room temperature

3 cups cooked pasta (6 ounces dry), plus ⅓ cup pasta cooking water (see note)

1 tablespoon snipped chives

I like to make this with medium-thick noodles—tagliatelle or fettucini—but any type of pasta will work well.

Fill a bowl with generously salted water, and set out a plate or bowl of crushed ice. Stick scissors into the puckered center of the urchin, and cut toward the outside. Then turn and cut in a circle, so you've just cut out the center of the top—it should look like a bowl with a bit of a curved lip. Discard the liquid in the center, then use a spoon to gently scrape out the uni—they'll run from the bottom center right up to the edge of the lip you created, so be gentle and try to get each of the five pieces out whole. Once you've removed a piece, rinse in the saltwater and lay it on the crushed ice. Give it a good shake in the water, but don't feel like you need to get every last speck off (it's mostly partially digested

THE PACIFIC NORTHWEST SEAFOOD COOKBOOK

seaweed). Repeat with the rest of the pieces. Your water might get murky, but it should still rinse fine.

Blend the urchin and butter together in a blender or mini food processor, then heat over low heat in a medium skillet. Add the pasta water. When it has come together, add the pasta. Remove from the heat and toss well. Salt to taste and garnish with snipped chives.

SALT AND PEPPER SQUID

SERVES 4 AS AN APPETIZER

Fried squid is a favorite in coastal towns around the world, but when it comes to making it at home, I find the light, cornstarch-dusted Chinese version to be easier to manage than the cornmeal-crusted Italian-American version. The frilly tentacles and crisp tubes in this recipe take on the spice and garlic of the second fry, making for an exciting dish—great for snacking or as part of a larger meal with rice and vegetables.

As with any type of frying, the key to squid is to get the oil super-hot and move quickly. You'll want to have everything completely ready to go, including two different pans, a heavy one for the deep-frying and a light one or wok for stir-frying, then work fast—but let the oil get hot again between batches.

1 tablespoon freshly ground
black pepper

1 teaspoon ground Sichuan
peppercorns

2 teaspoons kosher salt

1 cup cornstarch

1 pound squid, cleaned

3 cups peanut oil

1 small fresh chile pepper
(Serrano or similar), sliced
(remove the seeds for less
spice)

2 scallions, sliced, separate the
green from the white

2 garlic cloves, diced

2 tablespoons chopped cilantro

1 lime, quartered

Mix together the black pepper, Sichuan peppercorns, and salt. Mix about two-thirds of this into the cornstarch.

Pat the squid as dry as you can—this is one of the keys to the recipe, so take your time. Cut the tubes into ½-inch rings. Keep them separate from the tentacles.

Dredge the squid in the cornstarch mixture, making sure that you get every piece entirely covered—including inside the rings—then shake them off a bit to remove any excess.

Bring the oil up to 375°F in a large, heavy skillet over high heat. Set up a rack (ideal) or paper towel (less ideal, but who has a rack that holds squid?) for draining after frying.

Fry in four batches, two of rings and two of tentacles. Start with the rings. When you add the squid to the oil, it will bubble angrily. Use tongs or a metal spatula to keep all the squid submerged in the oil. Fry them for about 45 seconds, then flip and fry another 20. Transfer to the rack or paper towel. Repeat with the second batch of rings and both batches of tentacles. Sprinkle the remaining salt and peppercorn mix over the fried squid.

Add 2 tablespoons of oil to a wok or other large, light skillet over medium-high heat. When it gets hot, add the chile, scallion whites, and garlic, and stir as they cook. When they just begin to brown, turn the heat to high and add the squid and stir-fry—keeping all the food moving—for about a minute.

Transfer to a plate and toss with the cilantro and scallion greens. Serve immediately with the lime wedges for squeezing over top.

SQUID WITH SUMMER VEGETABLES

SERVES 4

HILLEL ECHO-HAWK | BIRCH BASKET CATERING | SEATTLE

Hillel Echo-Hawk, a member of the Pawnee Nation, grew up in the Upper Ahtna region of Alaska at the end of the Alaska Highway. This is where she learned how to forage and hunt, and developed her passion for cooking.

Today, Echo-Hawk runs Birch Basket Catering in Seattle, which focuses on pre-colonial food and education about Indigenous foodways, donating about half her time to contribute to the community and local tribes. While she, like most of us, is a guest on this Pacific Northwest land, she embraces the local foods—like geoduck and the squid, below—to prepare meals using pre-colonial ingredients.

3 ears corn

½ pound fingerling potatoes

4 tablespoons avocado oil

¼ teaspoon kosher salt, plus
　　more as needed

½ pound squid

½ yellow onion, sliced

¼ green bell pepper, diced

¼ yellow bell pepper, diced

¼ red bell pepper, diced

½ cup cherry tomatoes, halved

2 tablespoons chopped dill

Preheat the oven to 350°F.

Remove the corn kernels from their cobs. Set aside 1 cup of kernels (you can save the rest to make the Crab Esquites on page 139). Place the cobs in a pot and add just enough water to cover. Bring the water to a boil, then turn it down to a simmer for 30 minutes. Later, you'll use the water and discard the cobs.

While the cobs boil, cut the potatoes in halves or quarters—they should be about two bite-sized. Toss with 1 tablespoon avocado oil and ⅛ teaspoon of salt and put them in the oven until they're easily pierced with a fork, about 20 to 25 minutes.

Rinse the squid under cold water and cut the tubes into ¼-inch rings and the tentacles in half (vertically, so you don't have loose legs everywhere!). Pat the squid dry and place it in the refrigerator until ready to use.

Heat half of the corn over high heat in a medium sauté pan with ⅛ teaspoon of salt. Let it really char (3 to 5 minutes)—you'll need a pan big enough that they won't steam.

Heat 2 tablespoons of avocado oil over medium heat in a large sauté pan, then add the onion, cooking until translucent, about 6 to 8 minutes. Add the peppers and cook for another 3 to 5 minutes, until soft. Add the squid and let it sear—spread it out in the hot pan and just leave it—for about a minute, then stir and repeat. Add the tomatoes, dill, potatoes, salt, and both halves of the corn. Let it come together over the heat for 2 to 3 minutes.

Add 1 cup of the water from the boiled cobs to finish cooking the squid, about 2 to 3 more minutes. Taste and adjust the salt as needed, but be generous: it will help bring out the flavors of the corn and dill.

GRILLED OCTOPUS WITH SPRUCE OIL AND QUICK-CURED HUCKLEBERRIES

SERVES 4 TO 8 AS A LIGHT APPETIZER

SHEENA ELIZ

Seattle chef Sheena Eliz has worked in some of Seattle's best restaurants, including throughout the Mamnoon group, and while she doesn't yet have her own restaurant, with dishes like this that embrace the native ingredients in the Northwest, I hope she will someday.

The local octopus is bycatch, which means that nobody is out commercially fishing it—but when they do pull it up, they can keep it. The octopus ranges in size, but you'll want to aim pretty small for this—3 to 5 pounds is plenty (know that it looks huge, but it will cook down a fair amount). Occasionally you'll see them fresh at Pike Place Market, but you can often find them frozen at a fish market—and octopus is actually better when frozen, as it takes less time to tenderize.

3 cups kosher salt, plus more as needed

¾ cup fresh or thawed frozen huckleberries (blackberries work as a substitute), drained

One 3- to 5-pound octopus

1½ cups dry white wine

Spread about half of the salt on a baking sheet and scatter the berries on top. Pour the remainder of the salt on top, burying the berries. Refrigerate the berries while you prepare the octopus.

Remove the head from the octopus (or you can ask your fishmonger to do this for you) by cutting it off just below the eyes. The beak will stay in the middle of the tentacles and you can likely just remove it with your hands or a small knife, leaving you with just the tentacles. Rinse the octopus well.

½ cup plus 2 tablespoons extra virgin olive oil

1 yellow onion, halved

1 lemon, sliced, plus 1 cut into wedges for squeezing

1⅓ cups fresh spruce tips (if you can't find these, use fresh thyme)

Herbs of your choice to garnish (Sheena suggests purslane or chickweed)

Heat the wine, ½ cup of water, and 2 tablespoons of olive oil over medium heat in a heavy pot or Dutch oven. When boiling, turn it to a simmer and add the octopus, tentacles up. Curl each tentacle on top of the body. Add the split onion, sliced lemon, about 1 tablespoon of salt, and 1 cup of the spruce tips. Cover and simmer gently until tender, which varies wildly, but could be from 30 minutes to an hour and a half—estimate about 15 minutes plus an additional 15 per pound of octopus. You can tell it's done when you are able to pierce it with a fork. When it's finished, pull out the octopus and let it cool.

Heat ½ cup of olive oil and the remaining ⅓ cup of spruce tips in a small saucepan over low heat until fragrant, about 6 to 8 minutes. Turn off the heat and let it cool, then blend and strain.

Heat the grill or broiler to high heat.

Rinse and drain the huckleberries (you can rinse them pretty well: they'll keep their flavor while you remove the salt).

Cut the octopus into individual legs, salt them heavily, and grill or broil each leg until they're nice and charred. Slice the legs into thin pieces. Season them with the lemon wedges, salt (as needed), and an abundant drizzle of the spruce oil. Add the huckleberries and garnish with the herbs.

MIMOSA SARDINE SALAD

SERVES 4

The idea for this recipe comes from a local Russian immigrant friend of mine, who was telling me about mimosa salad, a layered salad made with canned fish. After a little research—and gawking at the cake-like presentation—it occurred to me that made with fresh sardines, which are already a bit oily, it could take on a bit of a lighter, more PNW flavor.

Likely you'll buy whole sardines to make this. You can either ask your fishmonger to fillet for you, or take them home and do it yourself (see sidebar).

1 pound whole sardines, cut into fillets (see sidebar)

1½ cups olive oil

¾ cup plus 2 tablespoons mayonnaise

2 carrots

4 eggs

2 Yukon gold potatoes

½ teaspoon kosher salt, plus more as needed

½ teaspoon freshly ground black pepper

½ red onion, diced and soaked for 15 minutes in water

2 tablespoons chopped dill

Salt the fish heavily on both sides and leave for 15 minutes. Rinse them and pat dry.

Heat the olive oil in a medium sauté pan over medium-low heat to about 120°F (below a simmer) and slip in the fillets for about 3 minutes. Remove the fish, reserving ¼ cup of the oil. Let the fillets cool, then chop them. Mix 2 tablespoons of the mayonnaise with the sardines.

Heat a large pot of well-salted water on high heat and boil the potatoes and carrots for 5 minutes, then add the eggs and continue to boil for 10 more minutes. Remove everything from the heat and let it cool.

Mix the ¾ cup of mayonnaise with the ¼ cup reserved sardine oil, and ½ teaspoon each of salt and pepper and set aside.

Peel the potatoes and carrots (the skins should slip off after cooking), and the eggs. Grate the potatoes in one pile, the carrots in another, and then the egg whites and yolks separately.

Now you're ready to assemble. Ideally, you'll do this in a trifle dish, glass baking dish, or a ring mold, so that the layers are visible—alternatively, you can do it in low glass jars and just make mini-versions. The size of the vessel doesn't really matter—in a smaller dish, you'll just have thicker layers.

Place the mayonnaise and oil mixture into a piping bag or plastic bag with a corner cut off. Spread the sardines along the bottom of the dish, filling up the horizontal space. Then do the same with a layer of the red onion. Using your piping bag, make a light layer of mayonnaise mixture (you can just make a bunch of crisscrossed lines, as spreading it will likely just mix it into the layer below). Add the grated carrot and a bit of salt, then another layer of mayonnaise mixture. Add the egg white layer, and again the mayonnaise mixture. Finally, add the potato (you may not want to use it all if your potatoes are large) and one more layer of mayonnaise mixture, before sprinkling the top with the egg yolks. Garnish with the dill and serve.

HOW TO FILLET SARDINES
Run the dull edge of your knife from tail to head on each side to remove the scales, then simply slice down the belly (directly opposite the spine). Remove the innards and then cut off the head and tail. Rinse and pat the sardine dry. Flatten the remaining body, skin side down, and feel for the spine. You should be able to pull it up easily. Some of the smaller bones may come with it, but if others remain behind, don't worry: they'll disappear in the cooking process.

CORNMEAL-CRUSTED SMELT WITH CAPER AIOLI

SERVES 4 AS AN APPETIZER OR 2 AS AN ENTRÉE

For many beginner or even advanced cooks, deep-frying is a frightening prospect: hot oil and high calories, for what? Some amateur sogginess. But when done right—as these instructions will show you—it gives a hearty crunch and big flavor to some little fish.

The frying does require a little extra effort, but that's negated by how little effort smelt require to prepare: just a rinse and a pat with a paper towel and you can fry and eat these smelt whole. If you or a guest is extremely squeamish about it, you can remove the head and innards, but the result of a lot of work is only slightly milder flavor and a much less good texture after frying. Besides, the cornmeal obscures what fish part you're eating.

To fry well, get everything you need ready before you start, use a pan with plenty of room, and know what you'll use to flip the fish and retrieve them. I find the best tools for this are chopsticks, but if you're not confident of your skills, small tongs or two forks work well, too.

½ pound smelt

1 cup buttermilk

Caper Aioli (recipe follows), for serving

1 cup peanut or vegetable oil

1 cup cornmeal

1 tablespoon hot paprika

Kosher salt, as needed

½ lemon, cut into wedges

After washing and patting dry, soak the smelt, whole, in buttermilk for 30 minutes. Prepare the Caper Aioli (recipe follows).

Start heating the oil in a wide pan over medium-high heat—you want it to be at least 350°F. Set up a rack or paper towels for draining after the frying step. Mix the cornmeal with the paprika and put half on a plate. Pull the smelt from the buttermilk, letting any excess drip off (though leave a little to help make the crust), and lay on top of the cornmeal, then cover with the remaining cornmeal. Make sure all the fish have a layer of cornmeal all around them.

Put the first fish into the fry oil. Make sure you get the loud sizzle that indicates it's plenty hot, then start adding more. Start with only about four fish at a time until you get a good rhythm.

As they brown, flip them over. Each fish will fry for about 90 seconds on the first side and a minute on the second. The fish cooks extremely quickly in the hot oil, so you don't need to worry too much about doneness—even a bigger fish, if that's all you can find, will fry by the time the outer crust browns.

Transfer the smelt to the rack. Don't pile or stack them, though—single layers will keep the crunch better. After each batch, sprinkle them with salt. Keep going until you've fried all the fish.

Serve with the lemon wedges to squeeze over the fish and the Caper Aioli for dipping.

CAPER AIOLI

¼ cup capers
2 garlic cloves
½ cup mayonnaise

While the smelt are soaking, use the side of a knife, a garlic press, or a mortar and pestle to smash up the capers and garlic. Mix both into the mayonnaise and set aside for dipping when the fish is ready.

ACKNOWLEDGMENTS

Without my husband, Brett, I would have died under a pile of seafood scraps, dirty dishes, and severe anxiety. His support while I wrote this book—both emotional and physical, by keeping the house clean and our children fed, bathed, and not harming each other—was invaluable.

Thank you, too, to those children, Jordana and Tove, for their (sometimes grudging) willingness to eat seafood pretty much every day for a year. Someday, they will either love or hate seafood, and when their friends ask why they have such strong feelings, the answer will be because I wrote this book in their toddler years.

Thank you to my mother, Shirley Bishop, whose endless edits, recipe testing, and childcare help were the only things that got me through the final months of writing this book. She withstood allergic reactions, burns, and my two-year-old complaining that her mac and cheese didn't have pickles on it (she's a big fan of the Dungeness crab version on page 146). Without my mom's help, I'd never remember to tell you when the skin stays on or off your salmon and the measurements might all be in "tabelpsoons."

Eternal and gorgeous gratitude to my photographer, Celeste Noche, who answered an inquiry about photography with an offer to do this book, who transformed my recipes into a vision, and who even stepped in to contribute a recipe of her own. Thank you to Rachel Knecht and Ari Koontz, who lent their cooking skills, food-lovers' eyes, and occasionally their hand-modeling expertise to the shoot.

On a similar note, thank you to Natasha Alphonse, whose stunning handmade ceramics show up in those photographs, and to Finex for lending their unique cast iron for the shoot.

To the chefs and cooks who gave of their knowledge and expertise by contributing a recipe for inclusion in this book: you are a big part of what shapes

Pacific Northwest seafood and how we eat it. Thank you for giving the rest of us an insight into how you do that.

And to my crew of testers, who helped make sure that every recipe in this book works: Amy Ferris Wheeless, Anna Berman, Annie Sullivan, Ben Bishop, Ben Grant, Brian Matheson, Cara Strickland, Chandra Ram, Chelsea Lin, Coral Sisk, Dalen Guieb, Dani Rustagi, Elise Evans, Emi Suzuki, Euryale Gadin, Frank Guanco, Georgia Freedman-Wand, Hanna Raskin, Hillary Hubacker, Jackie Varriano, Jenise Silva, Jenna Schnuer, Jessica Stugelmayer, Joshua Inoue, Julie Hubert, Kairu Yao, Kate Stern, Kate VanDerAa, Lauren Edlund, Lauren Garaventa, Leslie Devones, Lorraine Goldberg, Lyndsey Kleppin, Maia Paul, Marnie Devon, Martine Kaiser, Misty Shock Rule, Olga Berman, Rachel Belle, Rebecca Mongrain, Sandra Sullivan, Scott Migaldi, Sophie Squillaci, Tiffany Ran, Valentina Vitols, Venessa Goldberg, and Wendy Miller.

As a land-lubbing, boat-less fish lover, I must express my deep appreciation to the people who gave of their fish, shellfish, and fishing expertise, beginning with Eric Berto who, the minute this project was announced, dropped off a giant pile of fish for me to use in developing recipes. Also to Katie Goldberg and everyone with Alaska Seafood, Sena Wheeler at Sena Sea Wild Alaskan Fish, Shina Wysocki at Chelsea Farms, Amy Grondin, and, of course, Jon Speltz and Paula Cassidy, the owners of Wild Salmon Seafood Market, who put up with my daily questions and sometimes strange seafood needs.

Finally, thank you to my agent, Amy Levenson, who made this project happen, and to Aurora Bell and her team at The Countryman Press for making the process so smooth and beautiful.

INDEX

Italics indicate illustrations.

ABOUT THE AUTHOR

Naomi Tomky is the world's most enthusiastic eater of everything—and her passion for food is matched only by her love of her hometown of Seattle. She writes about food and travel for magazines, newspapers, and the internet. She won the Association of Food Journalists' 2016 Best Food and Travel Writing award and was included in *Best Food Writing 2017*. She has previously contributed to books, including *Fodor's Seattle* and *Lucky Peach's All About Eggs,* but this is her full-length debut. Learn more at naomitomky.com.

ABOUT THE PHOTOGRAPHER

Celeste Noche is an editorial and documentary photographer based in Portland, Oregon. Through her photos of food, travel, and portraits, she advocates for diversity and inclusivity, seeking to share stories of underrepresented communities. Her work has appeared on the BBC, *San Francisco Chronicle,* and *New York Times*. Find more of her work @extracelestial and celestenoche.com.